INDIAN PRAIRIE PUBLIC LIBRARY DISTRICT

3 1946 00223 9314

WITHDRAWN

JAN 24 2000

W9-ANW-892

INDIAN PRAIRIE PUBLIC LIBRARY
401 PLAINFIELD ROAD
DARIEN, IL 60561

Science Projects About the Environment and Ecology

Robert Gardner

Science Projects

Enslow Publishers, Inc.

40 Industrial Road	PO Box 38
Box 398	Aldershot
Berkeley Heights, NJ 07922	Hants GU12 6BP
USA	UK

http://www.enslow.com

INDIAN PRAIRIE PUBLIC LIBRARY
401 PLAINFIELD ROAD
DARIEN, IL 60561

Copyright ©1999 by Robert Gardner

All rights reserved.

No part of this book may be reproduced by any means
without the written permission of the publisher.

Library of Congress Cataloging-in-Publication Data

Gardner, Robert, 1929–
    Science projects about the environment and ecology / by Robert Gardner.
        p. cm. — (Science projects)
    Includes bibliographical references and index.
    Summary: Presents experiments and projects suitable for science fairs, dealing with
such aspects of the environment and ecology as the atmosphere, soil, water, plants,
animals, and climate.
    ISBN: 0-89490-951-7
        1. Environmental sciences—Experiments—Juvenile literature. 2. Ecology—
Experiments—Juvenile literature. 3. Science projects—Juvenile literature.
[1. Environmental sciences—Experiments. 2. Ecology—Experiments. 3. Experiments
4. Science projects.] I. Title. II. Series: Gardner, Robert, 1929– Science projects.
GE77.G37   1999
628'.078—dc21   98-35049
                                                                        CIP
507.862   AC

Printed in the United States of America

10 9 8 7 6 5 4 3 2

To Our Readers:
All Internet addresses in this book were active and appropriate when we went to press. Any
comments or suggestions can be sent by e-mail to Comments@enslow.com or to the address
on the back cover.

Illustration Credits: Stephen F. Delisle

Cover Photo: Jerry McCrea (foreground); © Corel Corporation (background).

Contents

*appropriate ideas for science fair project

*appropriate ideas for science fair project

Introduction

The science projects and experiments in this book have to do with the environment—the atmosphere, soil, water, plants, animals, and climate of Earth. For some of the experiments, you will need more than one pair of hands. In those cases, ask friends or family members to help you. Some of the experiments will take some time, so choose a partner who is patient. If possible, work with someone or some others who share your concern for the environment. In a few experiments **where there is a potential for danger, you will be asked to work with an adult**. Please do! The reason for the request is to prevent you from being hurt.

Like a good scientist, you will find it useful to record in a notebook your ideas, data, and anything you can conclude from your experiments. By so doing, you can keep track of the information you gather and the conclusions you reach. Using your notebook, you can refer to experiments you've done, and that may help you in doing future projects.

Science Fairs

Some of the projects in this book might be appropriate for a science fair. Those projects are indicated with an asterisk (*). However, judges at such fairs do not reward projects or experiments that are simply copied from a book. For example, a model of a leaf, which is commonly found at these fairs, would probably not impress judges unless it was done in a novel or creative way. On the other hand, a carefully performed experiment to find out how the removal of carbon dioxide from the air affects a plant growing under otherwise normal conditions would be likely to receive careful consideration.

Science fair judges tend to reward creative thought and imagination. However, it's difficult to be creative or imaginative unless you are really interested in your project. If you decide to do a project, be sure to choose a topic that appeals to you. Consider, too, your own ability and the cost of materials. Don't pursue a project that you can't afford.

If you decide to use a project found in this book for a science fair, you will need to find ways to modify or extend it. This should not be difficult because you will probably find that as you do these projects new ideas for experiments will come to mind. These new experiments could make excellent science fair projects, particularly because they spring from your own mind and are interesting to you.

If you decide to enter a science fair and have never done so before, you should read some of the books listed in the bibliography, including *Science Fair Projects—Planning, Presenting, Succeeding*, one of the books in this series. The references that deal specifically with science fairs will provide plenty of helpful hints and lots of useful information that will enable you to avoid the pitfalls that sometimes plague first-time entrants. You will learn how to prepare appealing reports that include charts and graphs, how to set up and display your work, how to present your project, and how to relate to judges and visitors.

Safety First

Most of the projects included in this book are perfectly safe. However, the following safety rules are well worth reading before you start any project.

1. Do any experiments or projects, whether from this book or of your own design, under the supervision of a science teacher or other knowledgeable adult.

2. Read all instructions carefully before proceeding with a project. If you have questions, check with your supervisor before going any further.

3. Maintain a serious attitude while conducting experiments. Fooling around can be dangerous to you and to others.

4. Wear approved safety goggles when you are doing anything that might cause injury to your eyes.

5. Do not eat or drink while experimenting.

6. Have a first-aid kit nearby while you are experimenting.

7. Do not put your fingers or any object other than properly designed electrical connectors into electrical outlets.

8. Never experiment with household electricity except under the supervision of a knowledgeable adult.

9. Don't touch a lit high-wattage bulb. Lightbulbs produce light, but they also produce heat.

10. Never look directly at the sun. It can cause permanent damage to your eyes.

1

Ecology and Environment

"When we try to pick out anything by itself, we find it hitched to everything else in the universe." John Muir (1838–1914), who wrote this in his book *My First Summer in the Sierra*, was an American naturalist. He spent much of his life convincing the public and the national government that forests should be protected and conserved. In 1908, President Theodore Roosevelt established the Muir Woods National Monument in California in recognition of Muir's efforts. Muir's words are essentially a definition of ecology. A more formal definition would be that ecology is the study of the relationship of living plants and animals to each other and to the environment. The environment is the natural surroundings in which organisms live. The environment of a city dweller, for example, is very different from that of someone who lives in a rural area.

An ecosystem consists of the plants and animals and their environment within a given area. A pond is an ecosystem. On a more general scale, the entire earth may be considered an ecosystem.

In many ecosystems, the only outside source of energy is the sun. Only plants that contain the green pigment chlorophyll can make food from that energy. They alone are able to combine water

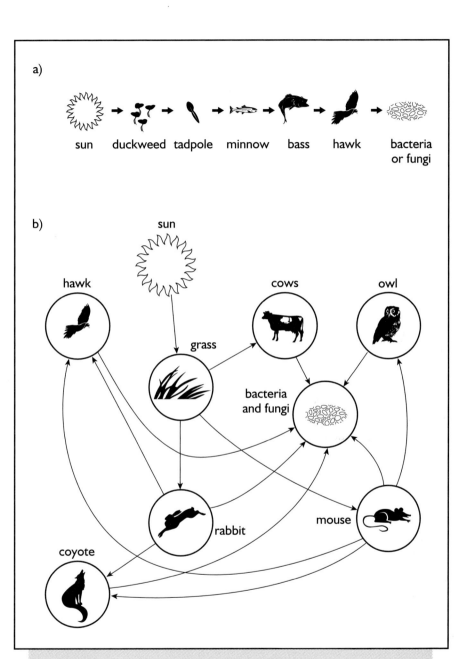

Figure 1. a) A food chain
b) A food web

and carbon dioxide to make food by a process known as photosynthesis. During this process, light energy is stored in the food as chemical energy. These plants are the primary producers in the ecosystem. The herbivorous (plant-eating) animals that feed on the plants are called primary consumers. Herbivorous animals include caterpillars, field mice, rabbits, and cows. Animals that eat the primary consumers are called secondary consumers. On what do you suppose tertiary consumers feed?

Some animals that eat only other animals, such as spiders, snakes, frogs, and wolves, are said to be carnivorous. Others are omnivorous; they feed on both plants and animals. Omnivorous animals include bears, raccoons, and chimpanzees. Are you herbivorous, carnivorous, or omnivorous?

The eating relationships among organisms within an ecosystem make up what is called a food chain. More accurately, the relationships form a food web because few consumers prey on just one plant or animal. Food chains or webs end with bacteria and fungi, as shown in Figure 1. These organisms, which lack the chlorophyll needed to manufacture their own food, are called decomposers. They absorb their nourishment from dead organisms. After the absorbed matter is digested by the decomposers, their waste products, such as nitrogen, carbon dioxide, and oxygen, are released into the air, water, or soil. Nitrogen-fixing bacteria that live in the soil and on the roots of legume plants such as beans, peas, clover, and peanuts change nitrogen gas, which makes up 78 percent of the earth's atmosphere, into nitrates. The water-soluble nitrates are absorbed by plants and converted into protein, one of the essential components of living tissue.

1-1*
The Diversity of Life in a Small Area

With the permission of the owner of a meadow or woodland, mark off a square meter or square yard of ground. With a hammer, drive stakes into the ground at the corners of the area you will examine. Then tie string to the stakes to surround the plot, as shown in Figure 2.

Record and describe, with drawings if you like, the various kinds of plants and animals you find within the area you have marked off. Field guides will help you identify what you find; however, it is not necessary to identify every

Things you will need:

- meadow or woodland
- hammer
- stakes
- string
- meterstick or yardstick
- notebook and pencil or pen
- shovel
- magnifier or dissecting microscope (optional)
- field guides (optional)

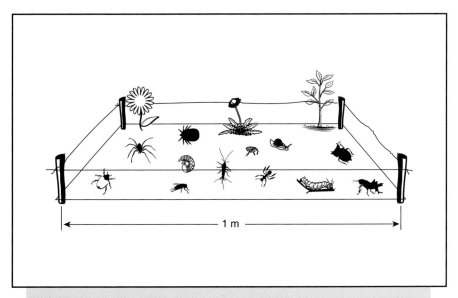

Figure 2. How many different living things can you find within one square meter of ground?

1 m

11

species. It is more important that you recognize the existence and relationships of the many different organisms you observe. Record, too, any other evidence of life that you find, such as feathers, seeds, fur, scales, and so on.

Again with permission, dig out a cube of soil about 10 cm on a side within your square meter of ground. Examine the soil carefully with a magnifier. What living organisms can you find in the soil? Are there worms? Insects? Snails? Seeds? Is there other evidence of living things? Make a list of all the living organisms you observed or found evidence of in the one-square-meter area.

Look closely at your list of living things. Which are producers? Which are consumers? Which are decomposers? Can you identify any primary consumers? How about secondary and tertiary consumers? Can you identify members of a food chain or food web? If you can, where do they fit into the chain or web?

Exploring on Your Own

With an adult to help you, carry out your own investigation of the various types of plants and animals in a pond and in the soil at the bottom of the pond. You will have to build devices that will allow you to capture and examine these life forms. **Do not go into or near the pond except under the supervision of an adult!** Return any life forms that you find to their original places.

1-2
Grasses and Weeds in Different Places

Things you will need:

- grasses and weeds from different microenvironments such as a lawn, along a fence, a pond, a meadow, a vacant lot, a forest, and a beach
- paper and pencil

Grasses and weeds are common plants, but there are many different species of both. To see whether location affects the kinds of grasses and weeds that grow, you can examine and compare these plants in different places. Look for these plants in a lawn, along a fence, near a pond, in a meadow, in a vacant lot, along the edge of a forest, near a beach, or in whatever other kinds of ecosystems you can think of. Notice whether each plant is growing in a sunny or a shady part of the habitat. For example, the plants growing on the south side of a fence might be different from those found on the north side. Was the ground where the plants grew dry, damp, or wet? Were certain animals, such as a distinctive insect, always found near a particular species?

It is not necessary to identify and name every different grass and weed species. You can simply make a drawing of each kind you see in each location, or cut a sample of each species you find. But be sure to record where each species was found and what details you notice about the location.

After completing your study, try to answer such questions as the following:

- Were any of the plants found in all the places you examined?

- Which plants, if any, were found only in certain places?

- Did some of the plants inhabit only sunny areas? Only shaded places?

- Were some plants found exclusively in damp or wet areas? Only in dry places?

1-3*
Finding Some Primary Consumers

Using 1-in x 2-in sticks, assemble a square wooden frame about 50 cm (20 in) on a side, as shown in Figure 3. **Wearing safety goggles**, nail the corners together. Stretch a piece of white cloth, such as a piece of an old bedsheet, across the frame. Use thumbtacks to hold the sheet or cloth firmly against the frame. Then turn the frame over so that the wood is on top.

Things you will need:
- four 1-in x 2-in sticks about 50 cm (20 in) long
- piece of white cloth about 50 cm on a side
- nails
- hammer
- safety goggles
- thumbtacks
- someone to help you
- tree branch with lots of leaves
- long stick

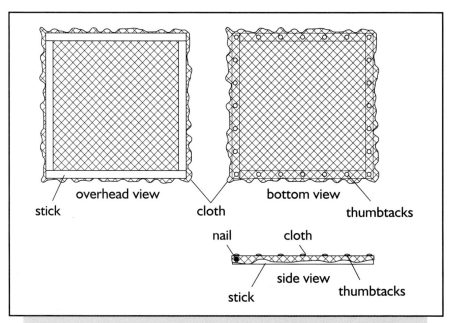

overhead view

stick

cloth

nail

bottom view

thumbtacks

cloth

side view

stick

thumbtacks

Figure 3. A piece of cloth attached to a square wooden frame can be used to collect some primary consumers.

14

Have someone place the frame under a tree branch that has lots of leaves while you whack the branch several times with a stick. You should see a number of primary consumers (and perhaps some other things) fall onto the white cloth. The frame will prevent any caterpillars and worms from crawling quickly away.

Can you identify any of the animals you find on the cloth? What secondary consumers might feed on the organisms you see on the cloth? Do you see any of these secondary consumers near the tree?

Exploring on Your Own

Compare the primary consumers you find on a tree branch with those on a bush. To capture the bugs in a bush, spread an old sheet under the bush. Then shake the bush a few times. How many primary consumers can you find on the sheet? How do they compare with the ones you found on the tree branch?

1-4*
The Rate of Photosynthesis and One of Its Products

As you know, primary producers can manufacture their own food by photosynthesis. Photosynthesis is the process by which plants combine carbon dioxide and water in the presence of sunlight and chlorophyll to make food. The food is sugar, which plants can store as starch. Another product of this process is oxygen gas. Living organisms, including you, need oxygen in order to obtain energy from food. They need energy in order to live and do things.

Oxygen makes up about one fifth of the air we breathe. It is needed to oxidize fuels such as wood, oil, and natural gas in a reaction we commonly call burning. You can use the fact that oxygen makes things burn (and in pure oxygen, they burn faster) to test for oxygen as a product of photosynthesis.

Things you will need:

• tape

• large nails or glass rods

• large jar or beaker

• water

• teaspoon

• baking soda

• small vial or medicine cup

• test tubes

• an adult

• sharp knife

• elodea, or pondweed (obtain from pond or store that sells aquarium supplies)

• string

• light source

• paper and pencil

• clock or watch

• wood splint

• matches

Rate of Photosynthesis and Light Intensity

Tape a large nail or glass rod to the outside of a large jar or beaker, as shown in Figure 4a. Fill the jar or beaker three-quarters full with water. Add a teaspoon of baking soda to the water and stir to dissolve the powder. The baking soda (sodium bicarbonate, $NaHCO_3$) will increase the amount of carbon dioxide in the water. The increased

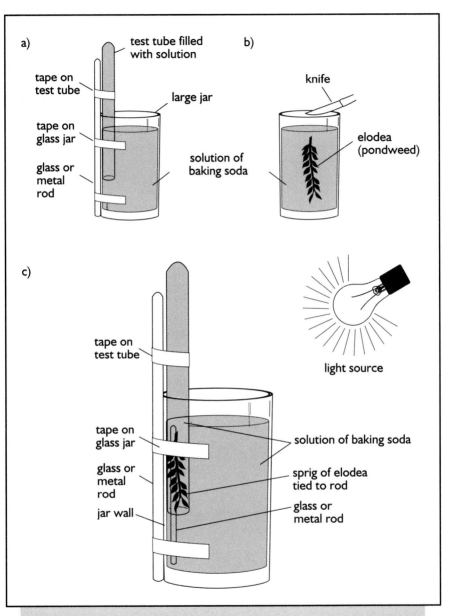

Figure 4. a) A test tube filled with baking soda solution is placed in a jar holding the same liquid. b) A sprig of elodea, or pondweed, is cut at an angle under the solution. c) The sprig is attached to a rod while under the solution and placed inside the test tube.

carbon dioxide will help you test the rate of photosynthesis. Use a small vial or medicine cup to scoop solution from the jar and pour it into a large test tube. When the tube is full, cover its mouth with your finger or thumb, invert it, and place it in the jar. Do not remove your finger until the mouth of the tube is submerged in the solution. **Ask an adult** to use a sharp knife to cut the stem of the sprig of elodea at an angle (Figure 4b). Be sure the stem is cut in the solution so that air cannot enter the plant.

Tie the sprig of elodea (still in the solution) to a glass rod or a large nail. Put the elodea, cut end up, into the lower end of the test tube. Then tape the test tube to the large nail or glass rod taped to the outside of the jar (Figure 4c). Place a light source near the jar. Adjust the distance between the light and the jar until the rate at which bubbles of oxygen emerge from the plant is about five per minute. Allow about five minutes for the rate to become steady. Once the rate is steady, count the number of bubbles released for three successive one-minute intervals. Record the average rate at which bubbles were produced with the light source at this distance.

Next, move the light source until it is half as far from the jar. What will this do to the intensity of the light shining on the plant? Again, allow five minutes for the rate to become steady, then record the number of bubbles produced during three successive one-minute intervals. What was the average rate at which bubbles were produced at this distance?

Repeat the experiment with the light at one fourth the original distance. What was the average rate at which bubbles were produced at this distance? How does the intensity of the light affect the rate at which photosynthesis takes place?

A Product of Photosynthesis

To be sure the gas produced is really oxygen, you can collect some and test it. Place several sprigs of elodea in the jar you used before. Cut each stem as before and cover the plants with a wide-necked

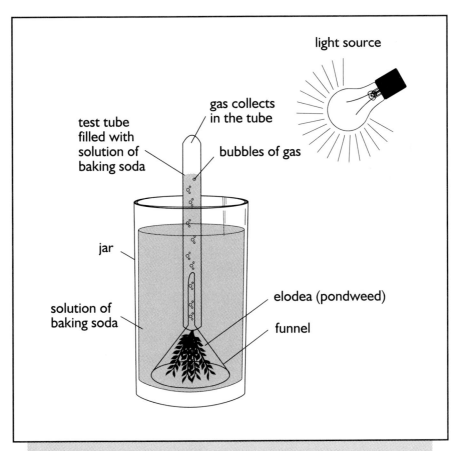

light source

gas collects in the tube

test tube filled with solution of baking soda

bubbles of gas

jar

solution of baking soda

elodea (pondweed)

funnel

Figure 5. The gas produced during photosynthesis can be collected in a test tube.

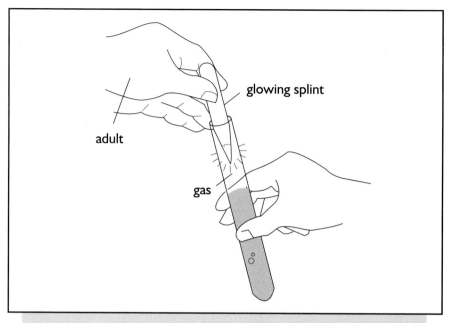

Figure 6. Ask an adult to lower a glowing splint into a test tube that contains the gas produced during photosynthesis.

glass or clear plastic funnel, as shown in Figure 5. The cut ends of the stems should be uppermost in the funnel. Fill a test tube with the solution in the jar as you did before. Place your finger over the mouth of the test tube and invert it. Then lower the test tube over the neck of the funnel. Bubbles of gas produced by the plants will collect at the top of the tube.

With the light source at the distance it was at the end of the last experiment, let photosynthesis continue until the tube is at least half filled with gas. You are now ready to test the gas to see whether it is oxygen. Cover the mouth of the test tube under water with your finger or thumb and remove it from the water. Turn the tube right side up, keeping your finger over its mouth. **Ask an adult** to light a wood splint. When the splint is burning well, have the adult blow out the splint and lower the glowing end into the test tube immediately after you remove your finger from its mouth (Figure 6). What evidence do you have that the gas you collected was oxygen?

1-5
Another Product of Photosynthesis

In addition to being our source of oxygen, primary producers are also the world's food source. They are the only form of life that can combine carbon dioxide and water to manufacture food. The process takes place only when light is present. Some of the light energy is transformed into chemical energy that is stored in the food. Photosynthesis takes place in leaves, because leaves contain the green pigment chlorophyll. It is this pigment that absorbs energy from white light. Leaves are green because chlorophyll absorbs most of the colors in white light; it reflects only the green portion of the light.

Things you will need:

- paper clip
- black construction paper
- geranium plant
- medicine cups or small vials
- eyedropper
- tincture of iodine
- water
- teaspoon
- cornstarch
- an adult
- gloves
- safety goggles
- tongs
- stove
- pan of boiling water
- alcohol
- small jar
- saucer

Excess sugar produced during photosynthesis is changed to starch and stored within the cells of the leaf. You can use the common test for starch (iodine) to confirm that food is produced in leaves. To carry out this test, use a paper clip to cover both sides of a geranium leaf with a small, folded piece of black construction paper, as shown in Figure 7. Be careful not to damage the leaf when you attach the paper. Do this in the morning on a bright sunny day when lots of light will fall on the geranium plant.

While the plant is bathing in sunlight, you can see how iodine reacts with starch. **Iodine is a poison. Never put it in your mouth!**

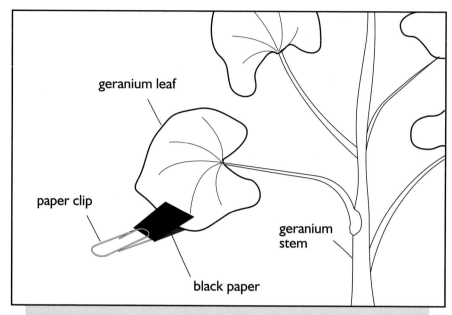

Figure 7. A paper clip can be used to attach a piece of black construction paper to a geranium leaf so that light cannot reach part of the leaf.

In a medicine cup, mix one drop of tincture of iodine with about 20 drops of water. Add a drop of the iodine solution to 1/10 of a teaspoon of cornstarch in another medicine cup or vial. What color appears when iodine is added to starch?

To see how you can test for the presence of starch in food, cut off a slice of potato and place it on a paper towel. Add a couple of drops of the iodine solution to the raw potato tissue (not to the skin). What evidence do you have that the potato contains starch?

After four to five hours, pick the leaf and its stem from the geranium plant and bring it indoors. Remove the clip and the paper. **Under adult supervision**, and while wearing gloves and safety goggles, grasp the leaf's stem with tongs. Then immerse the leaf into a pan of boiling water on a stove. Hold the leaf under the boiling water for about a minute. The hot water will break open cell walls within the leaf.

Next, you need to extract the green chlorophyll from the leaf so that any color changes caused by the iodine test can be seen. To do this, **first turn off the stove. Alcohol is flammable** and should never be brought near a flame or red-hot burner. Place the limp leaf in a small jar of alcohol and leave it overnight. The next morning you will find the alcohol has a green color due to the chlorophyll it has extracted from the leaf. In a saucer, mix together approximately equal amounts of tincture of iodine and water—about 5 mL of each will do. Next, rinse the leaf in warm water. Then spread it out and place it in the iodine-water solution.

What evidence do you have that starch was present in the leaf? Notice that one area of the leaf is much lighter than the rest. Can you identify that region? In which area of the leaf did photosynthesis not take place? How can you tell? What evidence do you have to indicate that light is required for photosynthesis?

1-6*
Plant Survival in Shade

You may wonder how plants, which depend on light to survive, are able to live in an environment where they are shaded by other plants or objects. Fortunately, plants respond to light by a process known as phototropism. To see what that means, plant a lima bean in each of two small flowerpots filled with garden soil. Keep the soil damp but not wet.

Things you will need:
- lima bean seeds
- 2 small flowerpots
- garden soil
- water
- 2 shoe boxes
- scissors
- cardboard
- tape or glue
- flat black spray paint

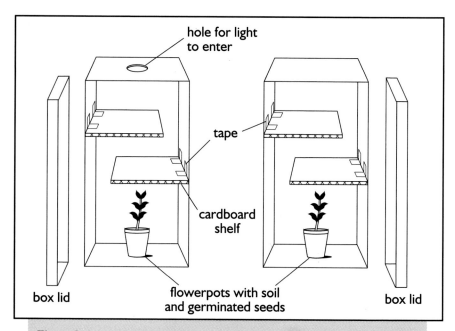

Figure 8. An experiment to test for phototropism is shown in this drawing. One box has a hole in the end so that light can enter; the other has no hole. The insides of both boxes are painted black. Once the lids are taped in place, light can reach only the plant in the box that has a hole in the lid.

For each of two shoe boxes, cut out two pieces of cardboard that are as deep as the box and about two thirds as wide. Tape or glue the cardboard pieces to the boxes as shown in Figure 8. You may want to make cardboard strips to provide support beneath the pieces of cardboard. Spray the insides of the boxes with flat black paint so that they are totally black. Cut a hole in one end of one box so that light can enter. Stand the boxes on end as shown. For the box with the hole, the hole should be at the top.

After the seeds germinate and the plants emerge from the soil, place each of them in a shoe box. Then tape the lids to the sides of the upright boxes. Remove the lids every other day to add water to the soil and to see how the plants are growing.

How does the growth of the plants in the two boxes compare? How would you define phototropism?

Exploring on Your Own

Do all plants exhibit phototropism? Design and carry out experiments to find out.

1-7*
Decomposers in the Soil

Soil contains a number of fungi and bacteria that will decompose many kinds of waste. Waste that can be broken down and returned to the soil as organic (carbon-containing) matter is said to be biodegradable. To find out the kinds of materials that are biodegradable, collect a number of things that you might throw away as trash or garbage. You might include an apple core, a banana peel, a cookie, lettuce leaves, tree leaves, grass clippings, pine needles, a chicken bone, a piece of paper, a plastic bag, an aluminum can, a tin (steel) can, and a Styrofoam cup.

Things you will need:
- waste items such as an apple core, banana peel, lettuce leaves, tree leaves, grass clippings, pine needles, chicken bone, paper, plastic, aluminum, a metal can, Styrofoam, etc.
- garden trowel
- wooden coffee stirrers
- large stone or concrete block
- decaying leaves
- plastic bag
- tray
- bright light
- magnifier
- forceps
- rotting logs
- rocks

Using a garden trowel, dig a small hole in the ground near your house for each of the items you collected. Be sure to obtain permission before you dig any holes. Use a wooden coffee stirrer to identify the location of each item after you bury it. Food items can be placed in one large hole and covered with a heavy stone or concrete block so that animals cannot reach them.

Every month or two, carefully uncover the items you buried. Which items decompose within a few months? Which items appear not to decay at all? Which substances do you think are biodegradable? Which do not appear to be biodegradable? What can be done with materials that do not decompose?

Go for a walk in the woods. Look for things that are undergoing decay. Can you find rotting leaves or pine needles? Look for them beneath newly fallen leaves and needles. Use a garden trowel to dig out some of the rotting leaves and a little of the soil beneath them. Place your diggings in a plastic bag and seal it.

Take the bag inside where you can examine the contents on a tray under a bright light. Use a magnifier and forceps to remove any animals you find. Can you find small roundworms? Earthworms? Insect larvae? Springtails? Ants? Spiders? Have you seen any of these animals in other places? When you have finished examining the animals in the decaying leaves and soil, return the contents of your bag to the woods.

Look under and inside rotting logs and under rocks. How can you tell when wood is decaying? What kinds of animal and plant life do you find? Are any of the animals the same as those you found in decaying leaves? Would you expect to find these same animals in a lawn or meadow?

Exploring on Your Own

Which do you think will decompose faster if buried in soil, a cotton sock or nylon hose? Design an experiment to find out.

INDIAN PRAIRIE PUBLIC LIBRARY
401 PLAINFIELD ROAD
DARIEN, IL 60561

1-8*
Watching Things Decay

Although you must be patient, you can watch the process of decay. Place some pieces of bread, tomato, and crackers in a clear plastic box that has a lid. Add a few drops of water to each item and put the lid on the box.

Things you will need:

• pieces of bread, tomato, crackers

• clear plastic box with a lid

• water

• moderately cool place

Put the box in a moderately cool place (12–18°C, or 55–65°F) where you can watch it. After a few days, you will probably see mold, bacterial colonies, and various other fungi growing on the food. Often the mold will produce tiny black spores that give the food a dark appearance. Molds reproduce by spores. Each spore can grow into a new mold and produce its own spores.

Continue watching. Can you see the food gradually disappear as it is consumed by the decomposers? **Be careful not to breathe in the mold spores or get them in your mouth! Do not do this experiment if you are allergic to mold.**

After you have collected your evidence, carefully discard the contents of the box into the garbage. Then, thoroughly clean the box and your hands with soap and hot water.

Exploring on Your Own

Food doesn't always decay. In fact, some foods can be kept for long periods and still be good to eat.

Find out how different kinds of food can be kept from spoiling.

Investigate the various methods used to preserve food. How does each method prevent food from decaying?

Will preserved foods ever decay?

28

1-9*
Water and Decay

Is water needed for things to decay? To find out, place a few dry foods such as a dry cookie, some dry cereal, and a piece of a dog biscuit in each of two plastic boxes. To one of the containers add enough water to dampen each food item. Add no

Things you will need:
- dry foods such as cookies, dry cereal, dog biscuit, etc.
- two plastic boxes with clear covers
- water
- a cool place

water to the second box. Put clear covers on both boxes and put them in a place where the temperature is moderately cool (12–18°C, or 55–65°F). Watch them over the course of several months. What do you conclude?

After you have collected your evidence, carefully discard the contents of each box into the garbage. Then, thoroughly clean the boxes and your hands with soap and hot water.

Exploring on Your Own

Design and carry out an experiment to find out whether or not light is needed for substances to decay. Based on your findings, what can you conclude about living organisms that cause decay?

Design and carry out an experiment to find out how temperature affects the rate at which food decays.

1-10*
Are Organisms Needed for Decay to Take Place?

Until the seventeenth century, people believed that small living organisms such as maggots, molds, and other fungi that appeared on decaying organic matter arose by spontaneous generation; that is, from nonliving matter. They believed the decaying matter itself spawned the life that fed on it.

Redi's Experiment

Francesco Redi (1626–1697) decided to test the idea of spontaneous generation experimentally. You can re-create and carry out his investigation, and then expand on it.

Redi's experiment is best done in the summer when flies are abundant. You will need six canning jars, which will not break when heated. **Ask an adult** to heat the open jars and their covers in a pressure cooker to sterilize them. Before you remove them from the pressure cooker, place two hot dogs in another pan of boiling water. After the hot dogs have cooked for a few minutes, cut them into six equal pieces. Put a piece of the recently cooked meat into each of the sterilized jars and quickly seal two of them by covering them securely with their lids so that nothing else can enter the sterile vessels. Cover the mouths of two other jars with

Things you will need:

- 6 canning jars with lids that can be sealed
- an adult
- pressure cooker
- 2 hot dogs
- pan
- water
- stove
- knife
- cloth gauze
- houseflies
- soap or detergent and hot water
- bouillon cubes
- measuring cup
- kitchen tongs
- masking tape
- marking pen
- spoon

gauze so that air can enter but flies can't. Leave the remaining two jars open so that flies can enter. Put the jars outdoors in a place where flies can reach them and leave them for several weeks. Observe each jar carefully on a daily basis.

In which jars do you find maggots? Can you find fly eggs in or on any of the jars? In which jars does the meat slowly decay? In which jars does the meat eventually rot as it is consumed by maggots? What can you conclude from your observations? Does spontaneous generation take place when food is protected from insects and mold spores?

After you have collected your evidence, carefully discard the contents of each jar into the garbage. Then, thoroughly clean the jars and your hands with soap and hot water.

Redi showed that maggots would not generate spontaneously on food. The maggots appeared only if flies could lay their eggs on the food. However, the spores of molds and other fungi can fall onto food even if it is covered by gauze, which flies cannot penetrate. Most spores cannot survive the temperature of boiling water, so the food in the sterilized sealed jars will remain unchanged.

In this experiment, you will see whether or not bacteria and fungi can form by spontaneous generation. Begin the experiment by dissolving a bouillon cube in 500 mL (1 pint) of warm water. What is the appearance of the bouillon? Leave the bouillon solution uncovered for a week. What is the appearance of the bouillon after a week? What evidence do you have that living organisms are in the bouillon?

Prepare a new solution of bouillon. Pour half of it into each of two one-pint sterile canning jars. Place the jars in a pan of water on a stove. **Have an adult heat the water to boiling**. Let the jars of bouillon and their covers sit in the boiling water for about 20 minutes. This should kill any spores that may have reached the bouillon. **Ask the adult to use tongs to remove the jars from the hot water**. When the jars are cool enough to handle, label them #1 and #2. Add a spoonful of the week-old bouillon broth to one of the new jars of bouillon. Add nothing to the second jar. **Ask the adult** to remove the lids from the hot water and place them on both jars, but don't seal the jars. Leave the jars where they can be observed daily. In which jar does the bouillon first show evidence of bacteria or fungi? What do you think prevents or greatly delays the growth of organisms in the other jar?

1-11
Yeast: A Decomposer

One decomposer that plays an important role in the economy is yeast. Yeast cells obtain their energy by changing sugar into carbon dioxide (CO_2) and alcohol in a process known as fermentation. Consequently, yeast is used to produce alcoholic beverages from sugars found in materials such as molasses and various grains. It is widely used in baking because the carbon dioxide it produces causes dough to rise (expand). Carbon dioxide is also used in many fire extinguishers because it is heavier than air, will not burn, and will not support combustion. The gas replaces air around a fire and puts out the flames.

Things you will need:

- spoon
- sugar
- dry yeast
- drinking glass
- water
- lid
- an adult
- match
- wooden splint
- test tube
- one-hole rubber stopper
- glass or hard plastic tubing
- soft plastic or rubber tubing
- limewater
- cooking oil
- drinking straw

To see that yeast can produce carbon dioxide, add a spoonful of sugar and a small packet of dry yeast to about one fourth of a glass of warm water. Stir the mixture and cover the glass with a lid. Within a few minutes you will see a frothy layer forming above the liquid. After several hours, remove the lid and most of the frothy layer above the solution. Swirl the liquid and put your ear near the glass. Can you hear gas bubbles being released from the solution? Place the lid back on the glass and wait several minutes. Then **ask an adult to light a wooden splint**. Remove the lid from the glass and have the adult lower the burning splint into the gas above the liquid, as shown in Figure 9a. What happens to the flame? What does this indicate about the gas produced when yeast acts on sugar?

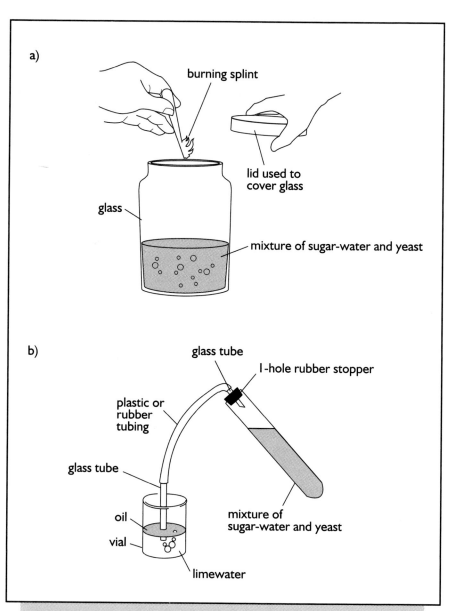

a)

burning splint

lid used to cover glass

glass

mixture of sugar-water and yeast

b)

glass tube

1-hole rubber stopper

plastic or rubber tubing

glass tube

oil

vial

mixture of sugar-water and yeast

limewater

Figure 9. a) Can you detect evidence of carbon dioxide when yeast and sugar are mixed in water? b) Does the gas produced from a mixture of sugar, water, and yeast react with limewater?

A better way to test for carbon dioxide is shown in Figure 9b. Put a small quantity of the same mixture of sugar water and yeast in a test tube. Place a one-hole rubber stopper with a short length of glass tubing in the tube's mouth. A length of plastic or rubber tubing will carry any gas released by the yeast and sugar water mixture to another piece of hard plastic or glass tubing that is immersed in a vial containing limewater. If you do not have any limewater, you can make some from the lime you buy at a garden or agricultural supply store. Just stir a teaspoon of the white solid into a small jar of water. Put a cap on the jar and let the mixture settle overnight. Pour the liquid into a second jar, leaving any white solid behind. Then screw a cover onto the jar. The limewater is covered with a thin layer of cooking oil to seal it off from the air, which contains a small concentration of CO_2. In the presence of CO_2, limewater will turn milky. Was CO_2 released by the yeast? How can you tell?

To see the milky substance that forms when CO_2 reacts with limewater, place a small amount of limewater in another clear vial. Using a drinking straw, blow into the limewater. **Do not drink the limewater**. About 4 percent of the air exhaled from your lungs is CO_2, enough to affect the limewater. Only about 0.04 percent of the air you breathe in is CO_2, so the concentration of CO_2 increases by about 100 times while in your lungs. Where does that additional CO_2 come from?

2

Cycles in the Global Environment

The substances essential to life—water, carbon, and nitrogen—form cycles that carry them through the atmosphere, the earth, and living organisms. With the exception of small amounts of matter that reach the earth as meteorites, the world's total mass of water, carbon, and nitrogen remains constant. Although the quantity and amounts of these substances in each phase of the three cycles remain relatively constant, they can be disrupted by the actions of humans. In this chapter we examine these cycles and see how they are affected by human actions.

The Water Cycle

Early scientists believed that the ocean's salt water was filtered within the earth to produce the freshwater found under the ground and in lakes and ponds. It was probably a French potter named Bernard Palissy (1510–1589) who first suggested that freshwater came from rainfall and not from the earth's core. But it was Edmond Halley (1656–1742), the English astronomer for whom a famous comet is named, who first made careful measurements to show that the earth's freshwater comes from rain.

Halley measured the rate at which water evaporated from the Mediterranean Sea. Using that figure, he calculated the total mass of water that evaporated from the Mediterranean in one year. He found that the mass of water evaporated per year was the same as the total mass of river water and rainfall entering the same sea each year. It was almost another century, however, before the idea of a water cycle became widely accepted among scientists.

Today we know that the world contains 1,370,000,000 cubic kilometers (328,000,000 cubic miles) of water. However, 97 percent of that liquid is in the salty oceans and is unfit for animals or plants that live on land. Another 37,500,000 cubic kilometers (9,000,000 cubic miles), which is 95 percent of the world's freshwater, exists as ice near the earth's poles. Table 1 reveals that only about 0.3 percent of the world's water is available for use by land-dwelling plants and animals.

Table 1: The amount of the world's water by location.

Location	Amount in cubic kilometers	Amount in cubic miles
Oceans	1,320,000,000	317,000,000
Polar ice caps	37,530,000	9,000,000
Underground (available)	4,170,000	1,000,000
Underground (unavailable)	4,170,000	1,000,000
Lakes and ponds	125,000	30,000
Soil	66,700	16,000
Atmosphere	12,900	3,100

Underground water is found in aquifers that lie beneath the earth's surface. They were formed by and are replenished by rainwater that seeps through the soil and fills the spaces between porous rock and gravel. All this water and soil rests on bedrock, which water cannot penetrate. In any given region, the top of this water-filled space beneath the ground is called the water table. Sometimes aquifers are stacked one above another and separated by soil or rock that water cannot penetrate (see Figure 10).

Wells, from which water can be pumped, are made by digging or drilling into aquifers. Some aquifers are so deep that their water is heated by the earth's hot inner core. If such aquifers have openings that reach the earth's surface, they are the source of hot springs or steam geysers. Cold-water springs are found where an aquifer's water table reaches ground level. Some aquifers empty into rivers, many of which, but not all, flow eventually to an ocean.

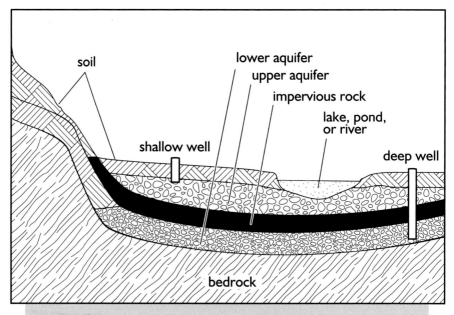

Figure 10. Underground water is found in aquifers. Sometimes aquifers are layered and separated by impervious rock (rock that water cannot penetrate). These aquifers may open to the earth's surface as springs.

Water flowing in rivers or in ocean currents provides visible evidence that water moves. But the motion of most of the world's water is upward into the air as invisible vapor. The vapor is produced by evaporation of water from the surface of the ocean, lakes, and rivers, as well as from the plants and soil that cover the earth's land. Evaporation brings water continuously into the earth's atmosphere, where 12,900 cubic kilometers of it is found (see Table 1). This gaseous water is in a constant state of flux, because it is the source of the water that falls back to earth as rain.

Figure 11 shows that in the earth's water cycle, 511,000 cubic kilometers (122,000 cubic miles) of water evaporate each year, mostly from the oceans. An equal amount condenses annually and falls as rain. A quarter of the rain falls on land, where it evaporates again or flows into rivers and aquifers. About 40,000 more cubic

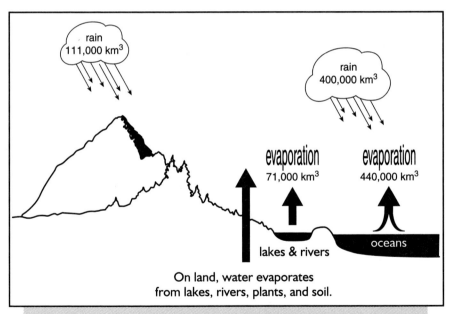

rain
111,000 km^3

rain
400,000 km^3

evaporation
71,000 km^3

evaporation
440,000 km^3

lakes & rivers

oceans

On land, water evaporates
from lakes, rivers, plants, and soil.

Figure 11. The earth's water is constantly evaporating from both land and bodies of water only to fall again as rain. If you add the numbers shown in the drawing, you will see that the total volume of water evaporating equals the volume that falls as rain.

kilometers of water evaporate from the ocean annually than condense and fall back as rain. The excess that evaporates falls as rain on the continents that make up the earth's land surfaces. Much of this water flows over and through the land back to the seas. The rest eventually evaporates again into the atmosphere.

A growing demand for water by the human population has reduced the level of many aquifers. Farmers in arid lands often remove so much water from rivers and aquifers to irrigate their crops that cities and other farmers farther away are faced with serious water shortages.

2-1
A Miniature Water Cycle

You can make a miniature water cycle to show how water moves from earth to the atmosphere and back again. To do so, place a small metal pan on a stove. Pour water into the pan until it is about half full. Use blocks of wood to support a larger pan above the smaller one, as shown in Figure 12. Add cold water and a few ice cubes to the upper pan. **Ask an adult to turn on the stove and heat the water** in the lower pan.

Things you will need:
- small, shallow metal pan about 20 cm (8 in) on a side
- stove
- water
- wood blocks
- large pan about 25–30 cm (10–12 in) on a side
- ice cubes
- an adult

After a few minutes, you will see tiny water droplets condensing in the air above the lower pan. Eventually, you will see water

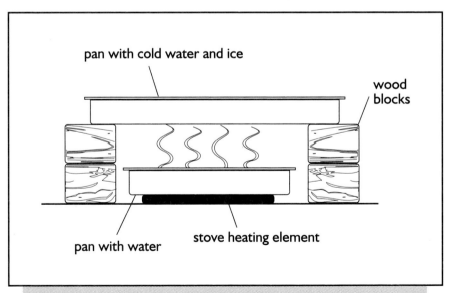

Figure 12. A miniature water cycle can be made by using two pans, water, ice, and a stove.

pan with cold water and ice

wood blocks

pan with water

stove heating element

condensing on the bottom of the upper pan. This water will form drops and fall back into the lower pan, which represents the earth's surface, be it land or water.

What does the upper pan represent in this miniature water cycle? In the real water cycle, what supplies the heat that causes the water to evaporate?

2-2*
Make a Cloud

The miniature water cycle in the previous experiment lacked the clouds we normally associate with rain. A cloud is made up of tiny water droplets that may come together (coalesce) and fall as raindrops. Clouds form because air pressure diminishes with altitude. Reduced pressure causes air to expand and cool. As the air cools, it may become saturated with water vapor. If tiny particles of ocean salt, dust, or smoke are present, the water vapor will condense around these particles as nuclei, forming droplets.

Things you will need:

- cold water
- bottle (about 500 mL or 1 pint)
- tire pump
- an adult
- one-hole rubber stopper to fit mouth of bottle
- rigid plastic tube to insert through hole in stopper
- rubber tubing
- flashlight or slide projector (optional)
- match

In the miniature water cycle you made in Experiment 2.1, there was no way to reduce the air pressure, so a cloud did not form. The water condensed instead on the bottom of the cold pan. Figure 13 shows how you can produce a sudden reduction in air pressure that will cause water vapor to condense.

Put enough cold water in a bottle to cover the bottom to a depth of about a centimeter (1/2 inch). **Be sure the bottle is not cracked!** Shake the bottle in order to saturate the air inside with water vapor. Attach a tire pump to a one-hole rubber stopper. **Ask an adult** to insert a rigid plastic tube through the hole in the stopper. A piece of rubber tubing can be used to connect the pump to the plastic tube. Push the stopper firmly into the mouth of the bottle. Then force air into the bottle with the pump. This will increase the air pressure inside the bottle. When the pressure blows the stopper out of the bottle, look for a cloud of condensing vapor in the bottle. The cloud

43

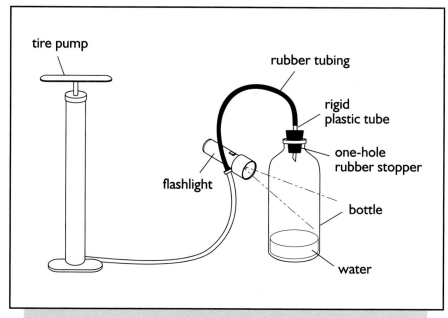

Figure 13. You can make a cloud in a jar if you suddenly reduce the pressure of the water-saturated air inside the jar.

is best seen outside in bright light. If you do the experiment inside, shine a flashlight or a beam from a slide projector through the bottle.

Did you see a cloud after the stopper popped out of the bottle? Probably not, because there were no tiny particles (nuclei) on which the vapor could condense.

Repeat the experiment, but this time **ask an adult** to light a match. Then remove the stopper, blow out the match, immediately drop the match into the bottle, and replace the stopper. The smoke particles will provide the necessary nuclei. Can you see a cloud now after the increased pressure blows the stopper out of the bottle?

Exploring on Your Own

Design another way to make clouds.

Investigate the conditions that produce clouds and rain in the atmosphere. Then see if you can predict when rain will fall.

The Carbon Cycle

Like water, carbon is an essential part of all living tissue. And carbon also moves in cyclical fashion from the air to living tissue, to the earth, and back to the atmosphere, as shown in Figure 14. Carbon, in the form of carbon dioxide gas, makes up about 0.04 percent of the earth's air. All foods—carbohydrates, fats, and proteins—contain carbon. Fossil fuels—coal, oil, natural gas—contain the carbon that made up part of the living tissues of plants and animals that lived millions of years ago.

Green plants manufacture most of the world's food from substances available in the earth's atmosphere and in the ground. Consequently, these plants play a vital role in the carbon cycle. During the process of photosynthesis, green plants combine the carbon dioxide in the air with water from the ground and from the air to make sugar. The sugar can be stored as starch in plant cells. Both plants and animals are able to synthesize protein, a basic component of living cells, by combining the carbon, oxygen, and hydrogen found in starch and other carbohydrates, as well as in fats, with nitrogen, sulfur, and phosphorus.

All living cells take in oxygen and release carbon dioxide, which enters the atmosphere or water. During daylight hours, more oxygen is produced by green plants than is consumed by respiration. At night, photosynthesis stops and cell respiration produces more carbon dioxide as oxygen is consumed. Carbon dioxide also enters the atmosphere when volcanoes erupt or when the organic (carbon-containing) matter in wood burns during forest fires. Over long periods, the atmospheric concentration of oxygen and carbon dioxide remain relatively constant. Oxygen constitutes about 21 percent of the atmosphere, nitrogen 78 percent, carbon dioxide 0.04 percent, and other gases about one percent.

When organisms die, their decomposition gives rise to carbon dioxide, which is released back into the atmosphere. Sometimes dead plants and animals get covered by other dead matter before decay is complete. As layers of this matter build up over millions of years, the pressure produces fossil fuels. In the case of oil, which lies in pockets deep inside the earth, the decay process results in hydrocarbons (liquid compounds made up of hydrogen and carbon). Natural gas is produced in a similar manner. Its hydrocarbons are smaller, lighter molecules such as methane (CH_4), ethane (C_2H_6), and propane (C_3H_8), which exist in the gaseous state. The other fossil fuel, coal, is a solid that is primarily the black element carbon. When fossil fuels are burned, they, too, produce carbon dioxide that is returned to the atmosphere.

Since the beginning of the industrial revolution, humans have had a decided impact on the carbon cycle. During the last century and a half, the concentration of carbon dioxide in the atmosphere has increased by nearly 30 percent from 280 ppm (parts per million) to 360 ppm. The rate at which carbon dioxide levels are rising seems

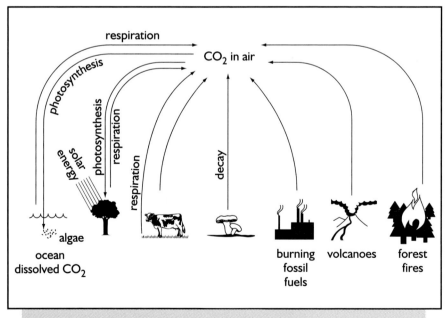

Figure 14. The carbon cycle is the movement of carbon from the atmosphere to the earth and back again.

to be increasing rapidly. Some scientists predict that atmospheric carbon dioxide will double during the next century.

Increased amounts of carbon dioxide in the air is the result of several factors. A growing population of humans and the animals needed to feed them has increased the amount of carbon dioxide entering the atmosphere through respiration. This is compounded by the recent cutting and burning of large tracts of the tropical rain forests. These forests absorb vast amounts of carbon dioxide during photosynthesis and release corresponding quantities of oxygen. As these forests are cleared for logging, mining, roads, and agriculture, the carbon cycle is affected because less carbon dioxide is removed from the atmosphere. Meanwhile, the burning of these forests adds more carbon dioxide to the atmosphere.

The major cause of increasing atmospheric carbon dioxide, however, is the use of fossil fuels to power electric plants, industries, and cars and to heat buildings. Our wide use of fossil fuels sends about 25 billion tons of carbon dioxide into the air each year. The increased level of atmospheric carbon dioxide raises global temperatures due to the greenhouse effect.

The Greenhouse Effect

The earth is constantly being bathed in sunlight. If all the sun's radiant energy that fell on the earth were retained and not reradiated into space, the earth would be too hot for life. On the other hand, if all that energy were reradiated into space each night, the earth would be too cold for survival. It is our atmosphere that acts as an insulating blanket, protecting us from the extreme temperatures that would make life impossible. During daylight, the atmosphere absorbs and reradiates about half the sun's energy. At night, carbon dioxide and water vapor in the air absorb the energy being reradiated by the warm earth and bounce some of it back to the earth.

A similar effect takes place in a greenhouse, hence the term *greenhouse effect*. The glass panes of a greenhouse transmit all wavelengths of visible light into the interior. However, the plants, soil, and other matter within the greenhouse absorb this radiation, then reradiate it as invisible infrared light. Infrared light has longer wavelengths (0.001–0.1 mm, or 0.0004–0.04 in) and less energy than visible light, and glass will not transmit infrared radiation. Consequently, the energy in the infrared light, which we sense as heat, is reflected back into the greenhouse. Much of the solar energy that entered the greenhouse as visible light cannot escape once it is reradiated as longer wavelengths. As a result, the heat and temperature within the greenhouse increase.

The earth is like a giant greenhouse. Its window is atmospheric carbon dioxide. As carbon dioxide levels rise, less heat can escape into space. Some scientists estimate that the earth's average temperature will rise by 3°C (5°F) during the next century. Such global warming may melt polar ice and cause a rise in sea level that will flood many coastal areas. Regions for growing crops will shift northward, temperate climates will become tropical, weather patterns will change, and storms will become more severe. The earth has undergone such temperature changes before as glaciers advanced and retreated across the globe. However, such changes took place over thousands of years so that plant and animal life could migrate slowly and adjust. Such changes took place also when the human population was minimal. Today, 6 billion water- and climate-dependent people inhabit the earth, and the number is growing.

2-3*
A Miniature Greenhouse

To see the greenhouse effect for yourself, find two identical outdoor thermometers that read the same. Tape a thermometer on the bottom of each of two identical flat pans or cardboard boxes, as shown in Figure 15. Tip the pans or boxes so that the shadow cast by one end of the box shades the thermometer bulbs. Alternatively, you can shade the thermometer bulbs with small cardboard covers. Leave one pan or box uncovered to serve as a control. Cover the opening of the other with plastic wrap. Use tape to fasten the plastic securely to the pan or box so that air cannot

Things you will need:

- 2 small identical flat pans or cardboard boxes
- 2 identical outdoor thermometers (-10–110°C)
- tape
- plastic wrap
- sunlight
- automobile

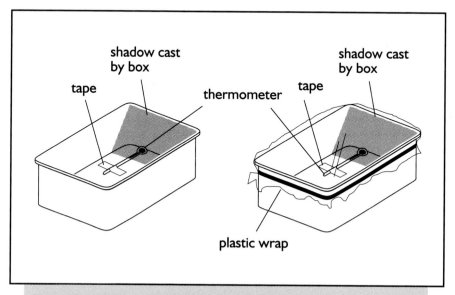

Figure 15. Place two pans, one open, one covered with plastic or glass, in bright sunlight. In which pan will the temperature rise?

49

enter or leave. Leave the pans in the sun until the temperatures in both stop changing. In which pan is the temperature higher? How can you account for any difference in temperature?

A car is a greenhouse on wheels. If you don't believe it, place a thermometer in a car that is sitting in the sun with all its windows closed. After about 20 minutes, open the door and read the thermometer. Roll down the car windows, wait another 20 minutes, and read the thermometer again. What evidence do you have that a car is a greenhouse on wheels?

Exploring on Your Own

Investigate other places where the greenhouse effect occurs as a natural phenomenon.

Does the greenhouse effect occur on other planets?

2-4
Decomposing with Heat to Find Carbon

In Chapter 1 you saw that substances can be decomposed by living organisms that obtain their energy from what we consider waste. But substances can be decomposed in other ways as well. In this experiment you will decompose matter by heating.

Find two aluminum pie pans. Make five shallow indentations about 2 cm (3/4 in) in diameter in each pan. Place small pieces of substances that you know decompose readily such as bread, cookie, apple, potato, and orange in the indentations of one pan. In the other pan place substances that appear to decay very slowly, if at all, such as sand, gravel, plastic, steel, and aluminum. Which pan contains substances that have living cells or substances that were once part of living organisms? Which substances can support the growth of organisms such as bacteria and fungi?

Ask an adult to place the pans on a stove and heat them. **Wearing safety goggles**, stay at least a meter (yard) from the materials as they are heated. Which substances decompose when heated? Which substances seem to be emitting steam? Which substances turn black? What do you think that black substance is? Did any of the materials that had a nonliving origin or that cannot support the growth of living organisms decompose? Did they form a black deposit? If they did, how can you explain their decomposition?

Things you will need:

- 2 aluminum pie pans
- substances that decompose readily, such as bread, cookie, apple, potato, orange, etc.
- substances that decay slowly such as sand, gravel, plastic, steel, aluminum, etc.
- an adult
- a stove
- safety goggles

The Nitrogen Cycle

Nitrogen is an element that makes up 78 percent of the earth's atmosphere. It is combined with other elements in all protein molecules. Protein is found in all living organisms and is one of the three basic foods, along with fats and carbohydrates.

In the nitrogen cycle, nitrogen moves from the air to the soil, back into basic living tissues, into the soil, and back into the air (see Figure 16). Certain microorganisms known as nitrogen-fixing bacteria are able to convert nitrogen gas to nitrates, which are soluble in moist soil. Some of these bacteria live in the soil. Others live symbiotically on the roots of legume plants such as clover, alfalfa, beans, and peas.

The nitrates in soil are absorbed by plants through their roots and used to make protein and other organic compounds essential to

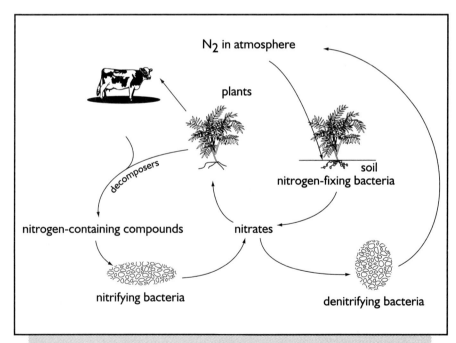

Figure 16. The nitrogen cycle involves the movement of nitrogen from the atmosphere to the soil, to living organisms, and back to the atmosphere.

life. These nitrogen-containing compounds are incorporated into the tissues of animals that eat the plants. The nitrogen compounds are transferred to other animals through food chains and webs.

Animal and plant wastes and remains are broken down by decomposers and converted to nitrogen compounds such as ammonium salts. These ammonium compounds are converted back to nitrates by other (nitrifying) bacteria, forming a subcycle within the nitrogen cycle.

Some of the nitrates in soil are acted on by denitrifying bacteria, which convert the nitrates back to nitrogen gas so that it reenters the atmosphere. Farmers try to prevent their fields from becoming soaked with water because denitrifying bacteria are abundant in waterlogged ground and remove nitrates from the soil.

The nitrogen cycle, like the carbon cycle, can be influenced by human actions. To provide the nitrates needed for good crops, farmers add chemical fertilizers such as ammonium nitrate (NH_4NO_3) to their fields. The nitrogen, which becomes incorporated in the plants, is removed when the plants are harvested. It is replaced with more chemical fertilizer at the beginning of the next growing season.

Rain often carries nitrates from the fields of farmers to nearby rivers, lakes, and ponds, where it can stimulate the growth of algae. Often the algae become so abundant that they blanket the water with a green cover, preventing light from reaching plants that grow below the surface and causing them to die. Respiring bacteria that feed on the dead water plants reduce the water's oxygen concentration. As the water becomes deficient in oxygen, it also becomes unfit for certain fish and other animals.

3

Humans and the Environment

In the previous chapter you learned that humans can affect the water, carbon, and nitrogen cycles. Unlike most other animals, humans are able to change and in many ways control the environment. We build homes to protect us from the elements, and we heat or cool these buildings to overcome the extreme temperatures provided by the natural environment outside. In order to heat these buildings, we burn fossil fuels and pour carbon dioxide and other pollutants into the air.

We do not hunt or gather our food from the environment; we buy it in packages at a store. Then we throw away the packages and some of the food in landfills, where it adds to an ever growing mound of waste.

There is no way that we can add to the earth's water, yet we take water for granted until a drought forces cities to raise water rates, ban the watering of lawns and gardens, and forbid car washing. The major use of water is to irrigate crops. But 75 percent of that water is lost to evaporation and transpiration. In some places, water for irrigation is drawn from aquifers at a rate greater than it is replaced by rainfall. The result leads to aquifers where the water table is continually dropping.

Our technology-oriented society is forever increasing its use of water. Bathtubs, hot tubs, dishwashers, clothes washers, flush toilets, sprinklers, swimming pools, and other water-hungry devices pull more and more water from a source whose yield cannot be increased.

In this chapter you will have a chance to investigate techniques to reduce the use of energy and water and generate less waste.

3-1*
Recycling Garbage

Much of what we throw away as garbage can be used. You would not want to eat it, but it can be used to make new soil for growing plants. Turning uneaten plant tissue into soil is called composting. A good time to start composting is in the spring as warm weather approaches.

Ask a parent or guardian for permission to dig a hole in a part of your yard that is seldom used. Dig out a cube of soil about 50 cm (20 in) on a side. Save the soil in a pile beside the hole. Cover the hole with a board so that animals cannot get into it and so that no one will fall into it.

After each meal, collect uneaten fruit and vegetable matter such as skins, peelings, apple cores, lettuce leaves, bread crusts, even coffee grounds. Almost any unused food except meat and bones, which produce a bad smell when they decompose, can be composted. Put this garbage in a plastic container. Each day, put the garbage you collect into a blender, add enough water to keep the blades submerged, and grind the garbage into small pieces. Pour the chopped garbage into the hole you dug and cover it with some of the soil you removed from the hole. Continue this process for about six weeks.

Cover the composting matter with a little soil and let it "stew" for two to three months. During that time, turn over the compost about every ten days. If the compost becomes dry, add water until it is moist.

After the compost has acquired a soil-like appearance, mix it one-to-one with some of the soil you dug from the hole. Add that

Things you will need:

- shovel
- a square board about 60 cm (2 ft) on a side
- unwanted fruit and vegetable matter such as skins, peelings, apple cores, lettuce leaves, and bread crusts
- plastic container
- blender
- water
- flowerpots
- flower seeds

mixture to some flowerpots. Put the regular soil you dug from the hole into an equal number of other pots. Label the pots so that you know which kind of soil (composted or regular) they contain.

Plant several flower seeds in each pot. Keep the soil in all the pots moist but not wet. After the seeds germinate, be sure both sets of plants receive equal amounts of water and sunlight. In which type of soil do you expect the flowers to grow better? Was your prediction correct?

Exploring on Your Own

Design and conduct an experiment to find out how the rate of decomposition of garbage is affected by the size of the composting particles.

Design and conduct an experiment to find out how the addition of small amounts of lime affect composting. You can buy lime at a garden or agricultural supply store.

Design and conduct an experiment to find out how the amount of water added to decomposing garbage affects the rate at which it changes to soil.

3-2*
Food in Packages and More Trash

A century ago, people obtained their food from their own land or from nearby farms. Food grown in the summer was stored in cellar bins, salted, smoked, or canned for use in the winter. Urban living has led to packaged food sold in stores to a society that resides far from the land that produces its meat, grains, fruits, and vegetables. Packaging not only increases the price of food, it adds to the waste we discard each day.

Things you will need:

• supermarket

• notebook and pencil or pen

• calculator

• variety pack of cereal

• single large package of cereal equal in weight to the variety pack

• balance or scale

• ruler

Does the price of a particular kind of food depend on the size of the package? To find out, use your notebook to record the prices of as many different packaged foods as possible. You might include different-sized packages of cereals, milk, juice, coffee, ice cream, potato chips, and meats. Note the weight or volume of each package. When you get home, calculate the cost per unit weight or volume of each type of food in each size package. (The cost per unit weight or volume is often referred to as the unit price.) For example, if a 13-ounce can of coffee costs $2.99, the price per ounce, or the unit price, would be

$2.99 ÷ 13 oz = $0.23/oz, or 23¢ per ounce.

If a 2-liter bottle of soda costs $1.49, the price per liter would be

$1.49 ÷ 2 L = $0.745/L.

This can also be expressed as 74.5¢ per liter or 0.0745¢ per mL, because there are 1,000 mL in a liter.

As the size of the package in which a particular type of food is sold increases, what happens to the unit price? Why do you think the unit price changes with weight or volume?

To see how packaging affects the price of food, note the cost of a variety pack of cereal that contains 8, 10, or 12 single-serving packages. Then note the cost of a single large package of one cereal in the pack that has approximately the same weight as the total weight of the variety pack. Which cereal in the variety pack is the most expensive? Which is the least expensive? Find one that is about average in price. How does the unit price of the average-priced cereal in the large box compare with the unit price of the variety pack?

If you can, buy the variety pack and a large box of the average-priced cereal. Save the packages as you eat the cereals. When all the packages are empty, weigh all the individual packages and the wrapping from the variety pack. Then weigh the large box. How do the two weights compare? How does the total surface area of all the small boxes in the variety pack compare with the surface area of the large box? What other factors account for the difference in unit price for these different ways of packaging cereal?

How can your choice of package size in buying groceries reduce the generation of waste?

Exploring on Your Own

Investigate some of the factors that companies consider when they design packages to hold the food or other products they sell. Is shape a factor? Color? How about the type of print on the package?

3-3*
Corrosion

Corrosion is one of the changes we commonly see in our environment. The corrosion of iron due to oxidation (rusting) is something you probably encounter every day. It is the reason many items are thrown away. To begin to find out what factors affect rusting, you will need three test tubes or three small, clear vials. Place a small finishing nail in each tube. Cover the nail in one tube or vial with tap water, cover a second nail with clear vinegar, and a third with clear household ammonia solution. Use tape and a marking pen to label the tubes or vials.

Test each solution by dipping one end of a strip of red and then blue litmus paper into the liquid. Remember that red litmus turns blue in a basic solution and blue litmus turns red in an acidic solution. Which liquids are basic? Which are acidic?

Things you will need:

- 3 test tubes or small, clear vials
- small finishing nail
- tap water
- clear vinegar
- household ammonia solution
- masking tape and marking pen
- red and blue litmus paper
- different metals such as steel, copper, aluminum, lead, zinc, brass, and bronze
- clear plastic box
- sponge
- safety goggles
- hammer
- 8 nails (not galvanized)
- 2 small boards
- paint and small brush
- cooking oil
- petroleum jelly
- heavy box or bucket
- stones
- aluminum and copper nails (optional)

After two or three days, examine the nails. Which nails, if any, show signs of corrosion (rust)? Pour off the liquids and let the nails dry. Reexamine the nails after they have dried. Which ones, if any, show evidence of corrosion? Does an acid appear to have any effect on rusting? How about a base?

Place pieces of different metals such as steel, copper, aluminum, lead, zinc, brass, and bronze in a clear plastic box along with a piece of wet sponge. Place the same metals in a second box that is dry (no wet sponge is added). Cover both boxes and leave them in a warm place where you can observe them for several months.

Which metals show signs of corrosion? What are the signs you notice? Does water appear necessary for corrosion?

Preventing Corrosion In and Out of Soil

Wearing safety goggles, use a hammer to drive four nails into each of two small boards. (Do not use galvanized nails!) Apply paint to one nail on each board. Cover a second nail on each set with cooking oil. Coat a third nail on each board with petroleum jelly. Do nothing to the fourth nail in each set. It will serve as the control. Use some of the paint to write a number on the board by each nail so that it can be identified. Bury the nails on one board by turning the board over and pushing the nails into the ground. Leave the second board of nails on top of the ground, above the one that is buried. Cover it with a heavy box or bucket and weigh it down with some rocks so that no one will step on the nails.

After about six months, pull up the board with the buried nails. Compare the nails on both boards. Which ones, if any, show signs of corrosion? Which of the materials used to coat the nails appear to provide the best protection against corrosion below ground? Above ground?

You might repeat the experiment, using coated and uncoated aluminum and copper nails. Do any of them corrode above ground? Beneath the ground?

Exploring on Your Own

If rusting is caused by oxidation, you would assume that rusting would not take place in the absence of air. Design and carry out an experiment to find out whether or not air (or oxygen) is needed for rusting to occur.

3-4*
Acid Rain

Things you will need:

- plastic containers
- pH test paper that can measure pH to at least 1/2 (0.5) a unit
- Internet and e-mail (optional)

Acidic soil, which affects corrosion, can be caused by the rain that falls on the soil. Gases such as sulfur dioxide (SO_2) and nitrogen dioxide (NO_2) are released from the smokestacks of many industries, such as coal-burning power plants. These gases dissolve in the water droplets found in clouds to form dilute sulfuric acid (H_2SO_4) and nitric acid (HNO_3). When these acids fall to earth as rain, they seep into the soil. They also fall on limestone and marble structures, which slowly dissolve in the weak acids. As the acid rain enters the soil, lakes, ponds, and rivers, it may kill the eggs and seeds of various animals and plants. This loss of life affects the food chains in these environments.

The strength of an acid is determined by its pH, which is a measure of its concentration of hydrogen ions (H^+). Neutral substances, such as pure water, have a pH of 7.0. Substances with a pH of less than 7 are acidic. Substances with a pH of greater than 7 are alkaline, or basic.

Actually, all rain is slightly acidic. The carbon dioxide found in the atmosphere is soluble in water and produces a solution that is slightly acidic. It is quite normal to find rain with a pH as low as 5.6. That is why acid rain is defined as rainwater that has a pH of less than 5.6.

To find the pH of rainwater, collect rain in plastic containers and test it with pH paper. Compare the color of the pH test paper dipped in rainwater with a standard found on the test paper container. The comparison will show you the rainwater's pH.

You will need to use test paper that can measure pH to at least 1/2 (0.5) a unit. That is, the paper should be able to distinguish pH 4.5 from pH 4.0 or pH 5.0. If your school does not have such test paper, you can buy it from a science supply house. A store that sells fish or swimming pool supplies will also have it.

Is the pH of the rain at the beginning of a storm different from the pH of the rain near the end of the storm?

Is the pH of rain affected by the season? Is it, for example, more acidic in the winter than in the summer? Is snow acidic? How can you find out?

Is the pH of rain affected by location? Is the rain in the eastern United States more acidic than the rain in the Midwest or the far West? If you or your school are connected to the Internet, perhaps you can find this information there. You might exchange e-mail with students in other parts of the country who could measure the pH of rain where they live.

Exploring on Your Own

What other substances contribute to air pollution? Design ways to detect some of these substances in the air.

3-5*
Coping with a Warm Environment

Most people sweat in hot weather. This is particularly true if a person exercises and produces more heat than usual within his or her body. Sweating is one way we cope with a warm or hot environment. This experiment demonstrates how sweating helps keep our bodies cool.

Soak a piece of thin cloth in lukewarm water. Squeeze out the excess water and wrap the damp cloth around the base of an outdoor thermometer, as shown in Figure 17. Use a rubber band to fasten the cloth to the thermometer. Once the thermometer reaches a constant temperature, hold it in front of a fan or take it outdoors and swing it through the air for about a minute. What happens to the temperature as the water evaporates?

Put one hand inside a plastic bag. Secure the open end of the bag around your wrist with a rubber band. Leave the other hand uncovered. Go outside or into a gymnasium and run around for a while until you begin to perspire. Which hand feels warmer? From which hand can your sweat evaporate? What evidence do you have that the evaporation of sweat has a cooling effect? Take off the plastic bag and wave that hand through the air. Does it begin to feel cooler?

Use your finger to make some liquid streaks on a flat piece of aluminum foil. Try making streaks with water, rubbing alcohol, and cooking oil. Which liquid evaporates fastest? Which liquid evaporates slowest? Which liquid do you think will feel coolest if it evaporates from the back of your hand?

Things you will need:
- piece of thin cloth
- lukewarm water
- 3 identical outdoor thermometers (-10–110°C)
- rubber bands
- electric fan
- plastic bag
- aluminum foil
- water
- rubbing alcohol
- cooking oil
- 3 identical aluminum pie pans
- newspaper or sheets of cardboard

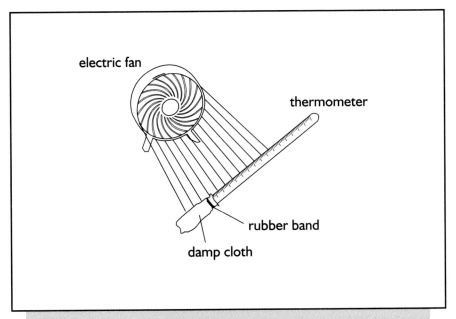

electric fan

thermometer

rubber band

damp cloth

Figure 17. What happens to the temperature when water evaporates?

Test your prediction by placing a little of each liquid, in turn, on the back of your hand. Which liquid makes your hand feel coolest when you wave it through the air?

To see how the rate at which water evaporates affects cooling, place equal volumes of hot water in each of three identical aluminum pie pans. Place the pans on folded newspaper or cardboard sheets to insulate them from the surface on which they rest. The pans should be several feet apart. Submerge identical thermometers in each pan and record the initial temperature in each one. To keep evaporation close to zero in one pan, add enough cooking oil to cover the surface of the water. Do nothing to the second pan. Increase the rate of evaporation in the third pan by creating a breeze across the water with an electric fan.

Record the temperature in each pan at one minute intervals for about half an hour. In which pan does the water cool fastest? In which pan does it cool slowest?

Exploring on Your Own

Design an experiment to see how evaporation rates are affected by temperature of the liquid, humidity, and surface area of the liquid. Why will you need at least two setups for each experiment?

Find out how an air conditioner works.

Design an air conditioner that does not require any energy input such as electricity.

3-6*
Coping with a Cold Environment

Color and a Cold Environment

The best way to cope with a cold environment is to wear plenty of clothes. But does the color of the clothes make a difference?

To find out, look for two shirts made of the same material: a white one and a dark blue or black one. Place both of them in sunlight on the same surface. Place identical thermometers inside the shirts, as shown in Figure 18. After a few minutes,

Things you will need:

- 2 shirts made of the same material, a white one and a dark blue or black one
- sunlight
- 2 identical thermometers (-10–110°C)
- hot tap water
- clear plastic cup with cover
- Styrofoam cups
- nail
- scissors
- clock or watch
- graph paper

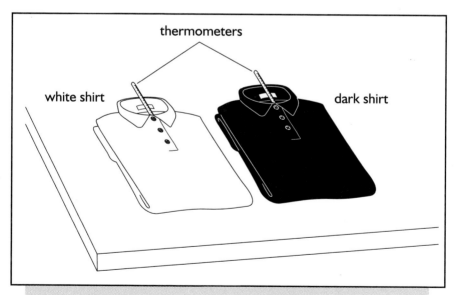

Figure 18. This drawing shows an experiment designed to see whether the color of clothing matters when coping with cold and warm environments.

read both thermometers. Should you consider color when choosing the clothes you need to cope with a cold (or warm) environment?

Different Insulating Materials

We wear clothes to reduce the rate at which our body heat escapes to the cooler environment. To begin to see how different materials can affect that rate, pour 150 mL of hot tap water into a clear plastic cup with a cover. Add an equal quantity of the hot water to a Styrofoam cup. Using a nail, punch a hole through the cover to accommodate a thermometer. To make a cover for the Styrofoam cup, use scissors to cut off the lower half of another Styrofoam cup (see Figure 19). Make a hole through the Styrofoam cover. Insert a thermometer through both covers. The bulbs of both thermometers should be well below the water level in the cups. Record the temperature of the water in each cup at 5-minute intervals over a period

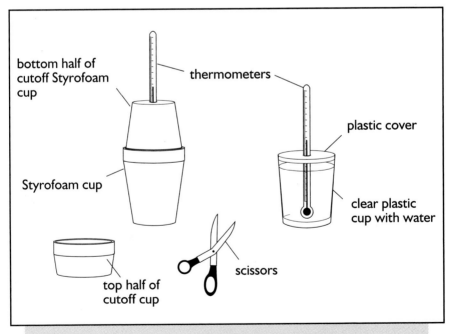

Figure 19. Will water lose heat faster through Styrofoam or through clear plastic?

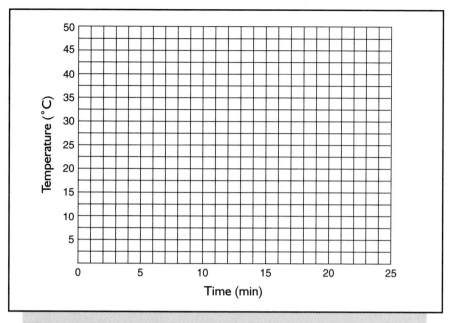

Figure 20. Plot your data on a temperature versus time graph like this one. In which cup, Styrofoam or clear plastic, does the water cool faster? Which cup is the better insulator?

of 30 minutes or more. If you have only one thermometer, you can do the experiment with each cup separately.

Use your data to plot a graph of temperature versus time (see Figure 20). You can plot the curves for both cups on the same set of axes. The two cooling curves provide a good comparison of the rate at which heat flows from the water in the two cups. Materials that reduce the rate that heat flows from a warm environment to a cooler one are called insulators. Which is the better insulator, clear plastic or Styrofoam?

Thickness of Insulation

To see how thickness of insulation affects heat flow, you can repeat the experiment and vary the thickness of the Styrofoam in two different cups. You can do this easily by making a second Styrofoam cup that is twice as thick. Simply place one Styrofoam cup inside another. Do the same for the cover.

Does the thickness of an insulating material affect the rate that heat flows through it? Cite evidence to support your conclusion.

Exploring on Your Own

Design and carry out experiments to test other insulating materials.

Design and carry out experiments to see how the temperature difference between the warm water and its surrounding environment affects the rate of heat flow.

Design and carry out experiments to see how the amount of the water's surface area affects the rate of heat flow.

3-7
To Cover or Not to Cover?

Pour 150 mL of hot tap water into each of two Styrofoam cups. Make a cover for one of the cups by using scissors to cut off the lower half of another Styrofoam cup (see Figure 19 in the previous experiment). Using a nail, punch a hole through what was the bottom of the cutoff Styrofoam cup. Insert a thermometer through the cover. Place another thermometer in the second cup, which will remain uncovered. The bulbs of both thermometers should be well below the water level in the cups. Record the temperature of the water in each cup at 5-minute intervals over a period of 30 minutes or more.

Things you will need:
- graduated cylinder or measuring cup
- hot tap water
- Styrofoam cups
- scissors
- nail
- 2 thermometers (-10–110°C)
- clock or watch with second hand
- graph paper
- cooking pan and cover
- stove
- an adult
- cold tap water

Use your data to plot a graph of temperature versus time. Based on the two cooling curves, does the cover reduce the rate at which heat flows from the water?

Will water heat faster in a pan that is covered than in a pan that is uncovered? Use the data you have just collected to make a prediction. Then, **under adult supervision**, measure the time it takes for equal amounts of cold water to reach the boiling point. Do the experiment first in an uncovered pan that holds a liter (or quart) of cold tap water. Record the time it takes to bring the water to a boil. After pan and burner have cooled to room temperature, repeat the experiment with a cover on the pan. You will know that the water is boiling when the cover starts jiggling. What do you find? Was your prediction correct?

71

Infiltration is the flow of cold outside air into a building through small cracks and openings, usually around windows and doors. It is particularly noticeable when a cold wind is blowing. Infiltration causes drafts that force warm air out through other openings, and it can be one of the major causes of heat loss from a building. Such leakage makes a building feel cold during the winter.

Things you will need:

- plastic wrap
- pencil
- tape
- fireplace (optional)
- an adult
- candle
- match
- caulk
- caulk gun
- weather stripping

A windy day is the best time to test for infiltration, because infiltration increases with wind velocity. Figure 21 shows two very easy

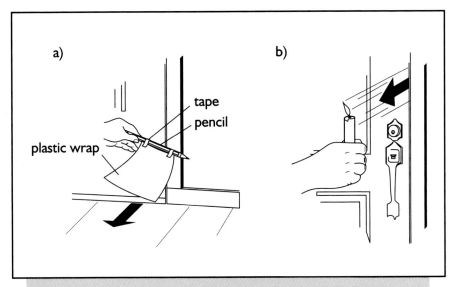

Figure 21. Two ways to detect infiltration are a) a simple plastic-wrap draft indicator and b) a candle flame.

ways to test for infiltration. One way is to simply tape one side of a piece of plastic wrap about 10 cm x 20 cm (4 in x 8 in) to a pencil. Hold the pencil near the edges of window frames and doors. The light plastic will move with any significant air currents. If you have a fireplace, be sure to check for air flow into the fireplace. How can you tell if the damper is open?

Alternatively, **under adult supervision**, you can move a lighted candle in the same way you did the plastic-wrap detector. Any infiltrating air will push the flame sideways. Once you locate air leaks, you will probably be able to feel them with the back of your hand, which is quite sensitive to temperature differences.

Having found the leaks, you can reduce infiltration by caulking cracks and installing weather stripping around windows and doors that leak air. If you have never done such jobs, work with a knowledgeable adult until you learn the technique. A few dollars spent on caulk and weather stripping can save hundreds of dollars in heating costs.

3-9*
Water Woes

As the world's population grows, more and more people must share the globe's unchanging volume of freshwater. Unfortunately, the growing number of people have contributed to increasing amounts of polluted water that cannot be used for

Things you will need:
• shower and bathtub
• ruler
• 2 calibrated plastic buckets
• recent bill from power company
• water meter or pressure gauge on water pump

drinking. In this investigation you will look for ways to conserve water, our most precious resource and one we cannot live without.

Shower or Bath?

Which requires more water, a shower or a bath? Let's assume a five-minute shower and a bath in which the tub is filled about halfway with water.

You can determine the water needed to take a bath in several ways. One way is to fill the tub halfway with water and then measure the water's average depth, length, and width. The product of those three dimensions will give you the water's volume. If you measure in metric units, remember that a liter of water is equal to 1,000 cubic centimeters. If you measure in English units, a gallon of water contains 231 cubic inches, and a quart about 58 cubic inches.

Another way to measure the volume is to take two plastic buckets that are calibrated in liters, quarts, or gallons. As water flows from the tub's faucet, collect it alternately in first one bucket and then the other before pouring it into the tub. You will have to keep track of the volume of water that enters the tub by counting or by having a partner record the volume of water in each bucket as you pour it into the tub.

How much water do you use in taking a bath?

To find the water needed to take a shower, turn on the shower for one minute. As it runs, collect water in alternate buckets, using the method described above for measuring bathwater. How much water would flow from the shower head in five minutes?

Which requires more water, a bath or a shower? How many times as much? How can this experiment help you conserve water? What else can you do to conserve water?

Heating Water

Bathing or showering not only uses water, a precious resource, but it requires hot water. Heating water requires energy. To see how much energy is needed, measure the temperature of the water that flows from your hot water tap. Then measure the temperature of the water that flows from your cold water tap. In both cases, be sure to let the water flow until the maximum or minimum temperature is reached.

How much energy, in calories, is needed to heat the water for a bath? For a shower? A calorie is the amount of heat needed to warm 1 gram (1 cubic centimeter) of water through 1°C (1.8°F). If you measured volume in gallons, a gallon of water contains 3,785 cubic centimeters of water. If you measured in quarts, a quart is 0.25 gallon.

To determine the electrical energy needed, which is measured in kilowatt-hours, you need to know that a kilowatt-hour is equivalent to 865,400 calories. Look at a recent bill from your power company to find out how much a kilowatt-hour of electrical energy costs. How much does it cost to take a bath if you heat your water by electricity? How much does it cost to take a shower?

If you heat your water with fuel oil or natural gas, how can you determine the cost of taking a bath or shower?

Regardless of the energy source you use to heat your water, why will your calculation of the cost of a bath or shower be less than the actual cost?

Leaks That Cost Money and Waste Water

A leaky faucet wastes water and money, but it is easy to detect. How can you determine the volume of water lost from a leaky faucet during a day?

Usually leaking faucets can be repaired by replacing a small washer inside the faucet. Some faucets are more complicated than others. Ask a knowledgeable adult to show you how to fix a leaky faucet. Once you know how, you can repair any leaky faucets in your house.

Some leaks may go undetected, but there are ways to tell whether or not you are losing water. If you buy your water from the city, there is a water meter at the point where water enters your home or apartment. Ask the members of your family not to use water during the night. After everyone is in bed, record the reading on the water meter. If you have your own well, check the pressure gauge on the water pump just before you retire. The next morning before anyone arises, check the water meter or the pressure gauge again. If the meter or gauge has the same reading as it did before you went to bed, you can be sure there are no leaks in the system. If the meter or gauge has changed, then water has flowed during the night. Water is leaking somewhere.

Perhaps it is an outdoor faucet, a toilet that leaks water, or a pipe that has a pinhole leak due to corrosion or a poorly soldered joint. See if you can find the leak and fix it.

Exploring on Your Own

About 6 gallons (23 liters) of water are used every time a toilet is flushed. Figure out a way to reduce the amount of water in the tank so that less water is used per flush. How much water does the reduced tank volume save per flush? Per month?

Think of other ways that your family can reduce their use of water. For example, water is wasted when a half-filled dishwasher is operated. If dishes are washed in the sink, you can show your family that less water is needed to wash the dishes in a pan than to let the hot water run throughout the dishwashing process.

Do some research on irrigation, which uses more water than any other activity. How can drip irrigation, which delivers water to the roots of plants, help reduce the world's demand for water?

4

Population and the Environment

The population of any species depends on many factors: disease; the number of predators; competition for food, water, and space; and changes in climate all affect the population of particular plants and animals. The population of any species increases when the number of births exceeds the number of deaths. It decreases when deaths exceed births.

The world's human population—the total number of people who inhabit the earth—is growing at an alarming rate. Because humans, to a large extent, are able to control their environment, the population has not yet exceeded its food supply—at least on a global level. However, as you have read in earlier chapters, global warming and the pollution of air, water, and soil may eventually halt the growth of the human population if humans don't voluntarily reduce their growing numbers.

4-1*
Gestation and Longevity

Mammals are animals whose young are born live and are nourished by their mother's milk. A mammal's gestation is the time between conception (the union of sperm and egg) and birth. Table 2 contains information about gestation and the average longevity (life expectancy) for a number of different mammals of increasing size.

Table 2: Gestation period and average longevity for a number of mammals of different sizes.

Mammal	Average gestation period (days)	Average longevity (years)
mouse	21	3
guinea pig	68	4
cat	63	12
fox	52	7
dog	61	12
deer	201	8
human	267	76
cow	284	15
horse	330	20
rhinoceros	450	15
elephant	660	35

Based on the information in the table, what happens to the gestation of mammals as the size of its species increases? In general, how is a mammal's longevity related to its gestation period? To its size? Why do you think human longevity is so much greater than the longevity of other mammals?

Exploring on Your Own

Investigate the gestation of animals not listed in Table 2. Do you still reach the same conclusions about longevity and gestation? About longevity and size?

4-2*
Population, Predators, and Prey

A predator is an animal that catches and eats other animals. The prey is the animal eaten by the predator. It is clear that the

Things you will need:

• Figure 22

• Figure 23

prey provides food for the predator, but does the predator provide anything for the prey?

Look at the graph in Figure 22. It shows the population of deer on the Kaibab Plateau in Arizona between 1890 and 1930. The plateau is surrounded by deep canyons, so few deer ever leave the plateau. The deer served as prey for mountain lions who also inhabit the area.

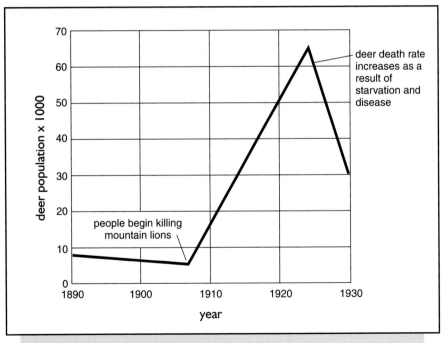

Figure 22. The deer population on the Kaibab Plateau between 1890 and 1930 is shown in this graph.

In 1906, as indicated on the graph, people began to kill mountain lions on the plateau. How did the reduction of the mountain lion population affect the deer population?

In 1924, as you can see from the graph, the deer population began to decrease rapidly, despite the fact that the population of mountain lions was still declining. It was found that the deer were dying primarily of starvation and disease, not because they were the prey of mountain lions. Why do you think the deer on the plateau began to starve? Think about what groups in the deer population would be most likely to die of disease or starvation. Which groups would be the most likely to be eaten by mountain lions?

Figure 23 shows the rabbit and lynx populations in a region of Canada between 1850 and 1930. Which of these two animals is the predator? Which is the prey? About every 10 years, the rabbits are ravaged by a recurring disease. How did the change in the rabbit population affect the lynx population?

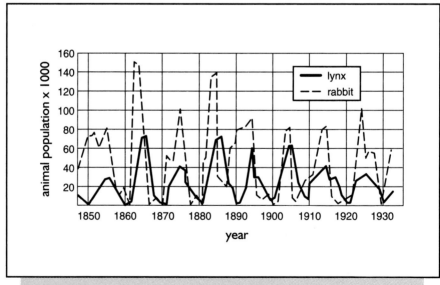

Figure 23. How does a change in the rabbit population affect the population of lynx in the same area?

Exploring on Your Own

How do you think the population of a particular plant species in a given area is determined? How do you think the population of a particular animal species in a given area is determined?

Determine the population of the dandelion plants in your lawn or the lawn of your school. How does the population change over the course of a year? Over several years? What factors affect this population?

Determine the population of a particular kind of wild animal in your town.

4-3*
World Population

Table 3 contains figures of estimates of the world's population since 2000 B.C.

Things you will need:
- graph paper
- pencil
- ruler
- calculator

Plot a graph of world population (on the vertical axis) versus time (on the horizontal axis) from 2000 B.C. to A.D. 1995. Leave room to extrapolate (extend) the graph to 2050. Draw a smooth curve through the points you have plotted. At what point in time did the human population begin to increase dramatically? What do you think might have caused this increase? What do you predict the population will be in 2050?

Make a second graph using just the data since 1900. Leave room to extrapolate (extend) the graph to 2050. Draw a smooth curve through the points you have plotted. What do you predict the population will be in 2050 according to this new graph? Which graph do you think gives you the best estimate for the population in 2050? Why do you think so?

Table 3: World population figures from 2000 B.C. to A.D. 1995.

Year	Population (in billions)	Year	Population (in billions)
2000 B.C.	0.15	1950	2.60
1 A.D.	0.25	1960	3.04
1650	0.55	1970	3.70
1750	0.73	1980	4.46
1850	1.18	1990	5.30
1900	1.60	1995	5.73

What do you estimate the population will be in 2010? Assume your estimate of the world's population in 2010 is correct. What is the difference between the population in 2010 and in 1995?

Now predict the population in 2010 by using the annual percentage or fractional increase in population. To estimate the annual fractional increase, divide the increase in world population between 1990 and 1995 (0.43 billion) by 5 years. Divide that number by 5.30 billion to find the annual fractional increase in population. Assuming the fractional increase remains constant, what will be the world's population in 2010?

You can use the y^x key on a calculator to estimate the world's population in 2010. Assume the fractional increase in population per year is 0.0162, which is an annual population increase of 1.62 percent. Then the population after one year will be 1.0162 times greater than it was the previous year. Enter 1.0162 into the calculator and press the y^x key, then press 20. That is the number of years between 1990 and 2010. Finally, press the equal sign. The number that appears is the ratio of the population in 2010 to the population in 1990. If you multiply the 1990 world population by the number on your calculator, you will have an estimate of the world's population in 2010.

What you are doing when you use the y^x key is finding the population after 20 years, assuming the annual rate continues at 1.62 percent. If the population is growing by 1.0162 times each year, then after 2 years it will be (1.0162 x 1.0162) or $(1.0162)^2$ times greater. After 3 years it will be (1.0162 x 1.0162 x 1.0162) or $(1.0162)^3$ times greater. After 20 years, which is the number of years we are interested in, the population will be $(1.0162)^{20}$ times greater. The calculator quickly multiplies 1.0162 by itself 20 times to find out what the population increase will be after 20 years.

How does the estimate made with the calculator compare with the estimate you made using the graph? Suppose the rate at which the population is changing increases before 2010. Will your estimate then be too high or too low? How will your estimate be affected if the rate at which the population is changing decreases before 2010?

At an annual growth rate of 1.62 percent, how long will it take for the population to double? In what year would we expect the world's population to be 10.6 billion?

Enter 1.0162, press the y^x key, then press the number representing your guess for the years required for the population to double. Then press the equal sign. If the answer is about 2.0, your guess was right. If not, try again until you get an answer of approximately 2.0.

In 1995, the population of the United States was 263.8 million and the birth rate was 15.1 live births per 1,000 people. The death rate was 8.7 deaths per 1,000 people. At what rate was the U.S. population increasing in people per 1,000? At what percentage rate was it increasing? At this rate, what will the United States population be in 2010? How long will it take for the United States population to double?

Exploring on Your Own

Find out how the figures given in Table 3 were obtained. How accurate do you think they are?

5

Energy and the Environment

Fossil fuels pollute our atmosphere and contribute to global warming through the greenhouse effect. Yet we depend on fossil fuels for heating buildings and producing much of our electricity. One source of energy that is free, constant, and nonpolluting is the light (solar) energy we receive from the our nearest star, the sun. Sunlight can be used to heat water and buildings and to produce electricity. Wind, another form of solar energy, is caused by uneven heating of the earth by the sun. As warmer air rises, cooler air flows in to replace it, creating air currents that we call wind.

Unfortunately, solar energy is diffuse, is present only when the sun is above the horizon, and may be greatly reduced by clouds. Despite these difficulties, scientists are working on ways to use sunlight and other forms of renewable energy in practical and economic ways. Until ways are found to provide the energy we need without polluting the environment, the best way to preserve our environment is to conserve energy.

In terms of scientific laws, we cannot avoid conserving energy. The conservation of energy is a fundamental law of nature: energy cannot be created or destroyed. Energy can be changed from one form to another, but the total energy remains the same. For example, an object resting at any point above the ground has potential energy; that is, it can do work if it is dropped. Should it fall, its potential energy is changed to kinetic energy (energy of motion). When the same object strikes the ground, its kinetic energy is converted to an equal quantity of thermal energy (heat). During photosynthesis, light energy is changed to the chemical energy stored in the food that is manufactured in plant cells. It is the energy stored in food that allows the consumer to carry out all the functions associated with life.

Instead of saying "conserve energy," which can be confused with what nature does through the laws of science, it might be clearer to say, "make use of as little energy as possible." Keeping buildings at 20°C (68°F) instead of 25°C (77°F); insulating the same buildings to reduce heat losses; driving smaller cars that use less fuel per mile; and using public transportation, walking, or biking instead of driving a car are all examples of things that can be done to reduce our consumption of energy.

5-1
Reducing the Use of Energy

A few ways to reduce energy use were discussed on the previous page. Because several minds are usually more productive than one, you might form a small group of people who are interested in reducing the use of energy or finding alternate energy sources for fossil fuels. Brainstorm within the group about ways to reduce energy usage or utilize energy sources that do not pollute the environment or contribute to global warming. You might begin by focusing on ways to reduce the use of electricity. From there you could move to methods for reducing heat losses from buildings, ways to reduce the use of gasoline, and the use of energy sources other than fossil fuels.

Things you will need:

• a group of friends

You will be surprised at how many ideas can be generated. But how many are practical? How can you find ways to put your ideas into effect in your own home? In other homes in your community? On a statewide, national, or international basis?

5-2*
A Miniature Solar Panel

You have probably seen solar panels on the south-facing roofs of buildings. The panels are used to convert light energy from the sun into heat. The heat is transferred to water or an antifreeze such as ethylene glycol, which is then pumped into the building, where it is used to heat air or water. In some cases, the solar energy is used to heat air directly; the air is then circulated through the building.

You can make a miniature solar panel like the one shown in Figure 24. Place some crumpled newspaper along the bottom of a cardboard box that is about 30 cm x 45 cm x 15 to 20 cm deep (12 in x 18 in x 6 to 8 in). The

Things you will need:

- old newspapers
- cardboard box about 30 cm x 45 cm x 15 to 20 cm deep (12 in x 18 in x 6 to 8 in)
- sheet of cardboard
- flat black spray paint
- several meters or yards of black rubber tubing
- large nail
- black tape
- plastic wrap
- table
- 2 buckets
- cold water
- chair, bench, or stool
- clothespin or large paper clip
- insulated cup
- thermometer (-10–110°C)

newspaper serves as insulation. Next, cut a sheet of cardboard to fit flat over the newspaper. There should be about 7 to 10 cm (3 to 4 in) of space above the cardboard.

Spray paint the inside of the box with a flat black paint. When the paint has dried, loop black rubber tubing on the cardboard sheet, as shown in Figure 24. Each end of the tubing should extend through holes you can make in the box with a large nail. Use black tape to hold the tubing in place. Cover the box with plastic wrap and tape the wrap securely in place. In addition to the black color, which absorbs solar radiation, you also have a miniature greenhouse (see Experiment 2-3).

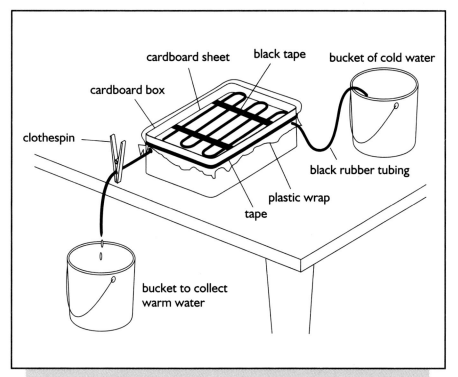

clothespin

cardboard box

cardboard sheet

black tape

bucket of cold water

black rubber tubing

plastic wrap

tape

bucket to collect
warm water

Figure 24. You can build a miniature solar collector that will heat water.

On a bright sunny day, place the solar panel in the sunlight on a table. Place one end of the tubing in a large bucket of cold water that also rests on the table. Lay the other end of the tubing on another bucket that rests on a chair or bench that is lower than the tabletop. Suck gently on the lower end of the tubing until water begins to flow through the tube. The difference in air pressure will cause water to siphon through the tubing from the upper to the lower bucket. When the water begins to flow, place a clothespin or a large paper clip on the lower tube to reduce the flow to a slow drip. After a few minutes, use your finger to compare the temperature of the water in the upper bucket with that of the water dripping from the lower tube. To make a more quantitative comparison, collect some of the warm water in a small insulated cup and use a thermometer to compare temperatures. What can you do to increase the temperature of the water emerging from the solar collector?

Exploring on Your Own

With adult help, build some real solar panels that can be used to heat water for use by your family or school.

5-3*
Electricity from Light

Solar (Photovoltaic) Cells

You may have a calculator that is powered by light (no batteries are needed). If not, you can probably borrow one or buy one for a very reasonable price. You will see that the calculator has a window below which are several small dark squares or disks. These thin, dark wafers are solar (photovoltaic) cells. They contain semiconductors that release electrons when light falls on them. The electrons give rise to an electric current that can serve the same purpose as one provided by a battery.

What happens if you cover the solar cells with your finger so that light cannot reach them?

Things you will need:

- calculator powered by solar cells
- solar cells
- an adult
- solder
- soldering gun
- safety goggles
- magnet wire
- tape
- small piece of wood
- galvanometer or milliammeter
- D cells
- voltmeter
- convex lens (magnifying glass)
- small piece of paper or dry leaf
- metal pan
- concave mirror (shaving or makeup mirror)

What happens if you partially cover the solar cells with your finger? Can you explain your observations?

You can buy one or more solar cells at an electronics store. The size does not matter. Handle solar cells with care. They are fragile. If the cells do not have electrical leads, **ask an adult** to help you solder two magnet wire leads to each cell. Wear safety goggles if you solder.

Once you have leads on the solar cell, it may be a good idea to tape its corners to a small piece of wood. This will make it easier to handle and reduce the likelihood of its being damaged.

91

Connect a solar cell to a sensitive meter. Depending on the cell, you may need a galvanometer or a milliammeter, which reads thousandths of an ampere. You can probably borrow one of these meters from your school. How does the current from a solar cell change when you shade part of it? How does it change as you vary the angle the cell makes with sunlight or some other light source? How should solar cells be oriented relative to the sun in order to operate at maximum efficiency?

Electrical cells, such as the D cells sold as flashlight batteries, can be wired in series (one after the other) or in parallel (side by side), as shown in Figure 25. How does the voltage of two D cells wired in series compare with the voltage across a single cell? How does the voltage across two D cells wired in parallel compare with

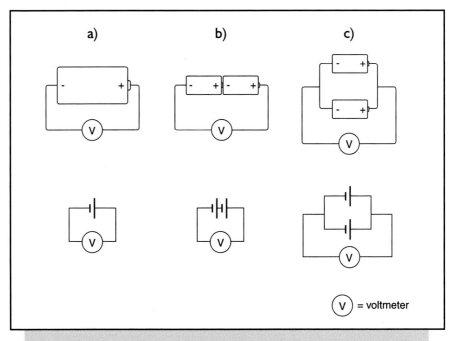

Figure 25. a) Two wires are used to connect a single D cell to a voltmeter. The lower diagram is a symbolic representation of the circuit. b) Two D cells are wired in series. c) Two D cells are wired in parallel.

the voltage across a single cell? Why do you think two or more cells might be wired in parallel?

Can you figure out a way to connect solar cells in series and in parallel? If you can, do they behave in the same way as D cells?

From Light to Heat to Electricity

Electrical energy is usually produced by giant turbines. These turbines are made to turn by water flowing over a dam or, more commonly, by steam. The steam is generated from the burning of fossil fuels or from atomic energy. But it is also possible to produce steam by heating water with sunlight. Of course, the sunlight must be concentrated. At Odeillo, Font-Romeu, France, sixty-three large mirrors that turn with the sun reflect sunlight onto a huge curved mirror. The mirror focuses the light onto a boiler, raising the temperature of the water inside the boiler to the boiling point. The steam generated is then used to turn a turbine and generate electricity.

To see how light can be concentrated to produce heat, **ask an adult** to watch as you use a convex lens (magnifier) outside to focus

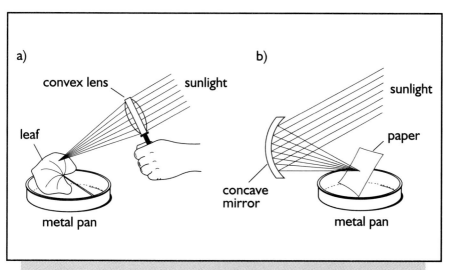

Figure 26. Sunlight can be brought together (so that the light rays converge) to produce intense heat using a) a convex lens and b) a concave mirror.

light on a small piece of paper or a dry leaf resting in a metal pan. Notice how the lens bends the parallel rays of light from the sun together to form a tiny circle of light on the paper or leaf (see Figure 26a). Can you make the paper or leaf burn?

In the generator in France, a concave mirror is used to focus the light from sixty-three mirrors onto the boiler. Shaving and makeup mirrors are concave mirrors that produce enlarged images of faces or objects held near them. These same mirrors can be used to bring light together as shown in Figure 26b. Using such a mirror to bring sunlight together, can you make a piece of paper or a leaf burn?

Exploring on Your Own

Concave mirrors used as shaving or makeup mirrors converge the light they reflect to a point of light, but concave cylindrical mirrors converge light to a line, as shown in Figure 27. Using cardboard, heavy wire, and aluminum foil, see whether you can build a cylindrical concave mirror that can be used to cook hot dogs with solar energy.

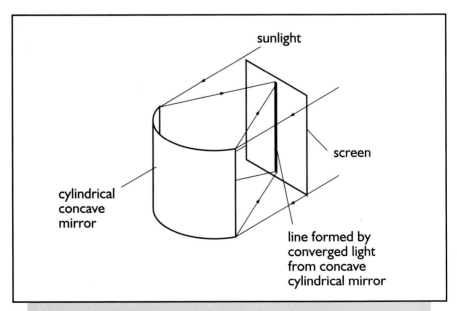

Figure 27. A cylindrical concave mirror will converge light to a narrow line.

Wind, another form of solar energy, can also be used to generate electricity. This is done on a large scale at huge wind farms in California. See whether you can design and build a model windmill that will generate small but measurable quantities of electricity.

The daily flow of ocean tides can also be used to generate electricity. Design and build a model tidal energy generator. What conditions are necessary for the construction of a practical power plant that can convert the flow of tidal water into electricity?

5-4*
Energy from Trash

Throughout much of the twentieth century, many towns and cities burned their trash and garbage or buried it in landfills. Burning waste added carbon dioxide and other pollutants to the air. Rain traveling through landfills carried toxic chemicals into underground aquifers, leading to the pollution of drinking water in wells and reservoirs. In many communities today, trash is separated into flammable and nonflammable components. Trash that will burn is then used in power plants to produce steam and generate electricity.

Things you will need:
- heavy work gloves
- week's worth of family's trash
- plastic bags
- balance or scale (bathroom scales are okay for large amounts, postage scale for small quantities)
- calculator
- ruler
- scissors
- an adult
- safe place to burn small amounts of trash
- cold water
- measuring cup or graduated cylinder
- 6-oz frozen juice can with metal bottom
- nail
- 2 bricks
- thermometer (-10–110°C)
- tongs or forceps
- matches

What's in Your Trash?

Put on a pair of heavy work gloves. With permission, go through the trash that your family throws away in one week. Separate it into categories that include paper and cardboard, plastics, yard wastes (grass, leaves, flowers, etc.), food, rubber and leather, glass, wood, cloth, metals, and miscellaneous. Place each type of trash in a separate bag and weigh it. What is the total weight of trash that your family throws away? Divide the total weight by the number of people in your family. How much trash per person per day does your family generate? How does it compare with the national average of about 2 kilograms (4.4 pounds) per day? **Wash your hands whenever you have handled garbage or trash, even if you wear gloves.**

What percentage of your family's trash is paper? What percentage fits into each of the other categories? What can be done to reduce the amount of trash your family throws away? For example, can any of the trash be recycled? Can clothes be taken to a thrift shop or donated to the poor? Hold a family meeting to explore ways to reduce the amount of trash generated in your home.

How Much Energy Can Be Obtained from Trash?

Having separated your trash into categories, take small samples from each kind of trash that will burn, such as paper, leaves, wood, and cardboard. Allow time for the materials to dry completely. Cut sample strips of paper about 3 cm x 10 cm (1 in x 4 in) from sheets of the waste paper. If you have access to a sensitive balance, determine the mass of one strip. If you have a less sensitive balance or scale, such as a postage scale, determine the mass of an entire sheet of paper. Estimate the mass of a strip by determining what fraction of a sheet it is. Use a similar method to determine the mass of small strips of cardboard, wood, leaves, and other flammable material.

To make a rough estimate of how much heat can be obtained by burning your flammable trash, ask an adult to help you. Find a place where you can safely burn small amounts of the trash. Then add 100 mL (3.3 oz) of cold water to a measuring cup or graduated cylinder. This much water has a mass of 100 g. Pour the water into an empty 6-oz frozen juice can that has a metal bottom. Place the can on two bricks, as shown in Figure 28.

Put a thermometer in the water and determine its temperature as accurately as possible. Now **ask the adult** to hold the paper trash you weighed with a pair of tongs or forceps. After the adult lights the paper with a match, have him or her quickly move the paper

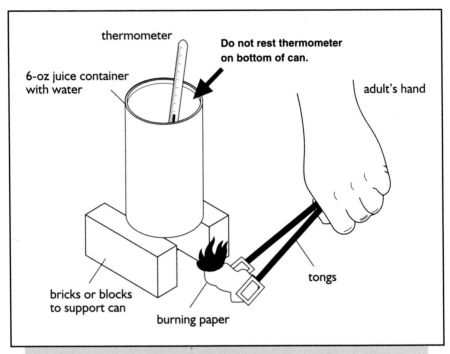

thermometer

Do not rest thermometer on bottom of can.

6-oz juice container with water

adult's hand

tongs

bricks or blocks to support can

burning paper

Figure 28. How much heat can be produced by burning a gram of flammable trash?

under the container of water. The heat produced by the flame will strike the container's metal bottom and be transferred to the water. After all the paper has burned, stir the water and read the final temperature. How many degrees did the water temperature rise?

As you probably know, heat is measured in calories. One calorie is the amount of heat needed to raise the temperature of one gram of water by one degree Celsius. Since you used 100 g of water, every Celsius degree of increase in the water's temperature means that 100 calories have been transferred to the water. How much heat was transferred to the water? This heat, of course, came from the burning paper. From the mass of the paper you burned, determine the heat released by the paper in calories per gram. Use this figure to determine the heat that could be obtained by burning all your paper trash.

Using a similar procedure, **ask the adult** to help you determine the heat that could be obtained by burning your other flammable trash. What is the total heat, in calories, that could be obtained by burning your trash?

Table 4 shows the heats of combustion (burning) for several different fuels. How does the heat per gram that can be obtained by burning your trash compare with the heat that can be obtained by burning the same mass of fuel oil, coal, natural gas, and wood?

Table 4: The heats of combustion for several common fuels.

Fuel	Heat of combustion in calories per gram
coal	6,600
fuel oil	11,000
methane	13,400
propane	12,100
wood	2,500

What is the population of your town or city? Assume that each person produces the same mass and kinds of trash as each person in your family. How much heat per day could be obtained by burning all the flammable trash in your city or town?

Exploring on Your Own

While burning trash for the energy needed to generate electricity reduces the amount of matter going into landfills and reduces the use of fossil fuels, it does have its shortcomings. Find out some of the reasons for not burning trash to generate electricity.

Solar energy, the tides, and burning trash can be used to replace fossil fuels, atomic energy, and falling water to generate electricity.

In what other ways can electricity be generated? Which of these ways are practical and environmentally safe?

In many communities, materials formerly regarded as trash are being recycled. How does recycling contribute to a better environment? What are some of the problems, both economic and practical, associated with recycling? Which materials are recycled in your town or city? Are there other materials that could be recycled? If so, why aren't they being recycled in your community? What happens to the materials that are recycled? Does your school recycle materials such as bottles, cans, and paper? If not, what can you do to encourage recycling there?

5-5*
Passive Solar Heating

Passive solar heating requires no mechanical devices to circulate warm or hot fluids. Solar panels found on roofs usually have one or more pumps to circulate water or air. Such systems are called active because they make use of mechanical devices to carry the heat absorbed from the sun.

In one form of passive solar heating, large, dark, concrete structures called Trombe walls are placed in front of south-facing windows. Other passive systems use large barrels filled with water or gravel to absorb heat. In these passive systems, the solar energy reaching the building during daylight hours is absorbed and stored so that it is available during the night and on stormy days, when the solar energy reaching the house is minimal.

Things you will need:

- 6 or more 8-oz cans without tops
- flat black spray paint
- water
- gravel
- sand
- dirt
- lead shot
- coal
- newspaper
- an adult
- conventional oven
- pot holder
- cookie sheet
- one or more thermometers (-10–110°C)
- south-facing window

To find out which materials might best serve as useful absorbers of solar energy in passive systems, you can paint six or more identical metal cans with flat black paint. Paint both the inside and outside surfaces of the cans. Fill the cans about three-quarters full with different substances. You might use water, gravel, sand, dirt, lead shot, coal, and newspaper. (Be sure to cover the water so that it won't evaporate.) **Ask an adult** to help you put all the cans in a conventional (not in a microwave) oven at 50°C (120°F) for about an hour. By that time all the materials should be at the temperature

101

of the oven. Use a pot holder to remove the cans and place them on a cookie sheet well away from the stove.

Use one or more thermometers to periodically measure the temperature inside the cans as they cool. Which substance cools fastest? Slowest? Which material do you think would be the best one to use to store solar energy? Can you explain why someone might choose to use a substance other than that one?

Allow all the cans to cool to room temperature. On a bright sunny day, place the cans in front of a south-facing window. Be sure they are arranged so that they all receive the same amount of sunlight. At the end of the day, record the temperature inside each can. Which material is warmest? Coolest? Do you think the warmest can holds the most heat? Why or why not?

Exploring on Your Own

Design and carry out an experiment to determine which material holds the most heat.

5-6
A Model Passive Solar-Heated Home

Using cardboard, wood, insulation, plastic wrap, tape, glue, nails, metal cans, and various other materials you think are appropriate, design and build a model passive solar home. Make use of what you learned in the previous experiment as well as new ideas of your own as you draw plans for your model. Once you have completed the plans, obtain the materials you need and construct the model.

Things you will need:
- cardboard
- wood
- insulation
- plastic wrap
- tape
- glue
- nails
- metal cans
- various other materials you think are appropriate
- pencil, paper, and ruler

Then, test it to see how well it works.

A good science experiment requires a control so that the experimental variable can be compared with the ordinary or normal mode or form. What might serve as the control in this experiment?

5-7
One Way to Conserve Electrical Energy

We all use electrical energy as a source of light. When you use a 100-w incandescent bulb for reading, you are using electrical energy, which is measured in kilowatt-hours (kwh). A kilowatt (kw) is 1,000 watts (w). A watt is a unit of power, and power is energy per time. A kilowatt of power is 1,000 joules per second (J/s), or 240 calories per second (cal/s). A kilowatt-hour, therefore, is 3,600,000 J of energy, because

Things you will need:

- electrical appliances such as a toaster, refrigerator, television set, and radio
- lightbulbs, incandescent and fluorescent, and their packages
- recent bill from power company

$$1,000 \text{ J/s} \times 3,600 \text{ s} = 3,600,000 \text{ J}.$$

Remember, an hour is the same as 3,600 s, because

$$60 \text{ min} \times 60 \text{ s/min} = 3,600 \text{ s}$$

If you measure energy in calories, a kilowatt-hour is

$$240 \text{ cal/s} \times 3,600 \text{ s} = 864,000 \text{ cal}.$$

If turned on for an hour, a 100-w (0.1 kw) lightbulb would require 0.1 kwh of energy:

$$0.1 \text{ kw} \times 1 \text{ h} = 0.1 \text{ kwh}.$$

If your power company charges you 10 cents per kilowatt-hour, it only costs you a penny to operate a 100-w lightbulb for one hour.

$$0.1 \text{ kwh} \times \$0.10/\text{kwh} = \$0.01 = 1¢.$$

Find the power rating of various appliances in your home. The wattage rating on lightbulbs is clearly written on the bulb. The wattages of various other appliances such as toasters, refrigerators, television sets, and radios are stamped on them, but you may have to look for the numbers. If you have to move the appliance to find the rating, ask an adult to help you.

For each appliance, estimate how much it costs to operate the device for a year. To do this, you will have to estimate the amount of time the appliance is used during a year. You will also have to know the cost of a kilowatt-hour of electrical energy, which can be found on your family's electric bill. Knowing the wattage rating of the appliance, the time it is used, and the power company's charge for a kilowatt-hour of electrical energy, you can calculate the cost of operating the device for a year.

For example, suppose your refrigerator is a 320-w appliance and you estimate that it is running about half the time. There are 8,760 hours in a year (24 hours/day x 365 days/year), so you estimate that the refrigerator runs 4,380 hours per year. If the power company charges 10¢ per kwh, then the cost of operating your refrigerator for a year is

$$0.320 \text{ kw} \times 4{,}380 \text{ h} \times \$0.10/\text{kwh} = \$140.16.$$

What is the yearly cost to operate some of the appliances and lightbulbs in your home?

Look carefully at the packages that contain incandescent and fluorescent lightbulbs. They indicate the number of lumens as well as the wattage of the bulb. The number of lumens is a measurement of the actual amount of light emitted. All electric lightbulbs, as you can tell by placing your hand near them (**do not touch a lit bulb**), emit much, or most, of the energy as heat. A baseball player's batting skill can be determined by calculating his or her batting average; that is, by dividing the number of hits by the number of times at bat. In the same way, you can determine how effectively a bulb converts electric energy into light. All you need to do is divide the number of lumens by the wattage to find the amount of light emitted per watt.

Do you obtain more light per watt from a low-wattage or a high-wattage incandescent bulb? Do you obtain more light per watt from a fluorescent or from an incandescent bulb? To conserve energy, should you use incandescent or fluorescent lights? Why?

Make a list of all the electrical appliances in your home. You will be amazed at how many there are. Some of them, such as electric clocks, shavers, and toothbrushes, require very little energy. Others, such as electric stoves, clothes dryers, air conditioners, and water heaters have very high wattage requirements. After you have made your list, try to think of ways that would reduce the total time that these appliances are in operation. Then estimate the savings that would result from reduced usage. Go to your family and show them your figures. Which of your suggestions will they agree to? Don't be surprised if some of your suggestions are rejected. Perhaps you can think of more practical approaches.

List of Suppliers

Carolina Biological Supply Co.
2700 York Road
Burlington, NC 27215
(800) 334-5551
http://www.carolina.com

Central Scientific Co. (CENCO)
3300 CENCO Pkwy
Franklin Park, IL 60131
(800) 262-3626
http://www.cenconet.com

Connecticut Valley Biological Supply Co., Inc.
82 Valley Road
P.O. Box 326
Southampton, MA 01073
(800) 628-7748

Delta Education
P.O. Box 915
Hudson, NH 03051-0915
(800) 258-1302

Edmund Scientific Co.
101 East Gloucester Pike
Barrington, NJ 08007
(609) 547-3488

Fisher Science Education
485 S. Frontage Rd.
Burr Ridge, IL 60521
(800) 955-4663
http://www.fisheredu.com

Frey Scientific
100 Paragon Parkway
Mansfield, OH 44905
(800) 225-3739

Nasco-Modesto
P.O. Box 3837
Modesto, CA 95352-3837
(800) 558-9595
http://www.nasco.com

Nasco Science
P.O. Box 901
Fort Atkinson, WI 53538-0901
(800) 558-9595

Sargent-Welch/VWR Scientific
911 Commerce Court
Buffalo Grove, IL 60089-2375
(800) SAR-GENT
http://www.SargentWelch.com

Science Kit & Boreal Laboratories
777 East Park Drive
Tonawanda, NY 14150
(800) 828-7777
http://sciencekit.com

Wards Natural Science Est.
5100 West Henrietta Road
P.O. Box 92912
Rochester, NY 14692-9012
(800) 962-2660
http://www.wardsci.com

Further Reading

Bonnet, Robert L., and Daniel G. Keen. *Environmental Science: 49 Science Fair Projects*. Blue Ridge Summit, Pa.: TAB, 1990.

Chandler, Gary, and Kevin Graham. *Alternative Energy Sources*. New York: Twenty-First Century Books, 1996.

———. *Protecting Our Air, Land, and Water*. New York: Twenty-First Century Books, 1996.

———. *Recycling*. New York: Twenty-First Century Books, 1996.

Coucher, Helen. *Whistling Thorns*. New York: Scholastic, Inc., 1993.

The Earth Works Group. *50 Simple Things Kids Can Do to Save the Earth*. Kansas City, Mo.: 1990.

Gallant, Roy A. *Earth's Vanishing Forests*. New York: Macmillan Books for Young Readers, 1992.

Gardner, Robert. *Celebrating Earth Day*. Brookfield, Conn.: Millbrook Press, 1992.

———. *Experimenting with Energy Conservation*. New York: Franklin Watts, 1992.

———. *Science Fair Projects—Planning, Presenting, Succeeding*. Springfield, N.J.: Enslow Publishers, Inc., 1999.

Hoff, Mary, and Mary M. Rodgers. *Our Endangered Planet: Groundwater*. Minneapolis: Lerner Publications, 1991.

Kerrod, Robin. *The Environment*. Tarrytown, N.Y.: Marshall Cavendish, 1993.

Morgan, Sally. *Ecology and Environment: The Cycles of Life*. New York: Oxford University Press, 1995.

Peckham, Alexander. *Resources Control*. New York: Gloucester Press, 1990.

Rybolt, Thomas R., and Robert C. Mebane. *Environmental Experiments About Renewable Energy*. Springfield, N.J.: Enslow Publishers, Inc., 1994.

Schwartz, Linda. *Earth Book for Kids*. Santa Barbara, Calif.: The Learning Works, 1990.

VanCleave, Janice. *Janice VanCleave's Ecology for Every Kid*. New York: John Wiley & Sons, 1995.

Woodburn, Judith. *The Threat of Global Warming*. Milwaukee, Wis.: Gareth Stevens, 1991.

Internet Addresses

The Envirolink Network. *Envirolink*. n.d.
    <http://www.envirolink.org> (November 16, 1998).

Environmental News Network. 1998.
    <http://enn.com:80> (November 16, 1998).

National FFA Organization. *Future Farmers of America*. 1998.
    <http://www.agriculture.com/contents/FFA/index.html>
    (November 16, 1998).

Voyage Publishing. *Science and the Environment*. 1996.
    <http://www.cais.com/publish> (November 16, 1998).

Index